D1212642

Geneses, Genealogies, Genres, and Genius

European Perspectives

European Perspectives

A Series in Social Thought and Cultural Criticism
Lawrence D. Kritzman, Editor

European Perspectives presents outstanding books by
leading European thinkers. With both classic and
contemporary works, the series aims to shape the
major intellectual controversies of our day and to
facilitate the tasks of historical understanding.
For a complete list of books in the series, see pages
v–vii.

Geneses, Genealogies, Genres, and Genius

The Secrets of the Archive

Jacques Derrida

Translated by Beverley Bie Brahic

Columbia University Press
New York

Columbia University Press
Publishers Since 1893
New York

Copyright © 2003 Éditions Galilée
English translation copyright © 2006 Beverley Bie Brahic
Originally published in France by Éditions Galilée, 9 rue Linne,
75005 Paris
All rights reserved

Library of Congress Cataloging-in-Publication Data
A complete CIP record for this book is available from the
Library of Congress
ISBN 0–231–13978–0 (cloth)

The publishers thank the French Ministry of Culture – National
Book Centre – for kindly granting a translation subvention.

Columbia University Press books are printed on permanent and
durable acid-free paper.
c 10 9 8 7 6 5 4 3 2 1

European Perspectives
A Series in Social Thought and Cultural Criticism

Lawrence D. Kritzman, Editor

Foreword

'What is called literature'

What is literature for Derrida? There are numerous texts to which one could turn in order to answer this question, each text perhaps offering different (if complementary) answers. A recent response comes in the essay on the university, 'The Future of the Profession or the University without condition (Thanks to the "Humanities" what *could take place* tomorrow)'.[1] Here Derrida states:

> I will call the unconditional university or the university without condition: the principal right to say everything, whether it be under the heading of a fiction and the experiment of knowledge, and the right to say it publicly, to publish it. The reference to public space will remain the link that affiliates the new Humanities to the Age of

Enlightenment. It distinguishes the university institution from other institutions founded on the right or the duty to say everything, for example religious confession and even psychoanalytic 'free association'. But it is also what fundamentally links the university, and above all the Humanities, to what is called literature, in the European and modern sense of the term, as the right to say everything publicly, or to keep it secret, if only in the form of fiction.[2]

Literature is then affiliated to the more-than-critical-deconstructive-unconditionality of the new Humanities by 'the right to say everything', publicly, published, 'if only in the form of a fiction'. Literature is thus one of those rare spaces which stands in a non-submissive, non-competitive relation to the sovereignty of power (the state, capital, the media, religion). The unconditionality of Literature is a space in which nothing is beyond questioning and commentary, including the mode of thinking that takes the form of questioning and commentary. Literature is in other words a space in which the impossibility of the democracy-to-come might be possible. It is the event of a deconstruction, a deconstruction as that which happens. Of course, there is what Derrida calls elsewhere 'the literary apparatus'[3] to be reckoned with, namely all the institutional powers which render a work as 'Literature' before it has ever been written (publishing houses, media review, bookshops and markets, the university syllabus and so on). However, to think literature as such an unconditionality is to re-imagine the literary from the ground up, free of every such prosthesis to which it has been subordinate in its modern sense but which are not necessary to it. The literature that Derrida refers to here is a deconstruction-as-more-than-Literature, just as the university without condition is not reducible to the managerialisation and appropriation of knowledge that passes under the name of the university today. This unconditionality is not a 'pure' literature or an uncontaminated university that exists somewhere beyond the tainted present or buried within the contaminated now. Rather, it is what Derrida refers to in this text, 'Geneses, Genealogies, Genres and Genius', following Hélène Cixous, as the 'Omnipotence-other' [*Tout-puissance-autre*] of Literature.

'What is called Literature . . . if only in the form of fiction' draws an undecidable line between the secret as absolute secret and the phenomenal appearance of the secret as such. Literature offers the secret at the same time as jealously guarding the secret (not in the form of an encryption that is potentially knowable but as an absolute deprivation of the power to choose between reality and fiction). Literature allows one to read at the same time as denying the power to read (in the sense of a determinable or saturable interpretation). Literature presents the right to read while simultaneously disconnecting that right from any position of authority that would determine or govern the reading. It does all this in the form of an event in which denied the authority to *read*, one can only read, and so yield to the otherness of reading as the arrival of what may come in the form of a fiction. That is the arrival of the secret, 'the other as that which happens', as Derrida puts it here (p. 51). This is the genius of literature, the infinite power to keep the secret undecidable and sealed from what it says even as it is publicly avowed. Literature is then the very space of the secret, the point at which literature itself begins and the place in which the secret has the chance of occuring. Thus, when Derrida speaks of the public space (the important term here rather than, say, 'fiction') and of literature, enlightenment and the unconditional university this is not a simple matter of an unrestricted or uncensored right to publish (although it is also this). It is, rather, the almost impossible tightrope walk which discriminates between the power of the sovereignty of the public and mediatic space in which literature arrives and the power of the powerless unconditionality of literature as a submission to the 'ominpotent' or 'all-powerful' otherness of the secret. Literature then, like a university without condition, would present something of a challenge to sovereignty because it is unmasterable. Rather, the undecidable in literature refuses sovereignty its own ipseity, rendering the sovereign divisible and no longer sovereign. This power is not a counter-force to the sovereign but the activity of the passive 'what happens' of the all-powerful, powerless other. Literature cannot be mastered, nor does it give up its secrets, just as it avows publicly that which cannot be avowed. Such strength in utter weakness is the genius of literature, which no power, no sovereignty, can ever over-come.

The figure, 'literary personality', who perhaps more than any other exemplifies this situation today is, for Derrida, Hélène Cixous. A 'genius' [*une génie*] of every literary genre (the theoretical essay, the novel, the theatre, the poetic) and a 'genie' of the university-without-condition (as teacher and public person), her work, the extraordinary hyper-text which operates under the name of Hélène Cixous, presents a considerable disturbance to all the forces of sovereign mastery. I mean this not in terms of what might be considered the relative banality of public pronouncements or the occasion of publication by Cixous (although it is also this) but rather in the sense of a body of work which so remarkably wrenches, retrenches and deFrenches the French idiom. If, as the expression goes, one can speak of the genius of a language as the potential of its grammatical and semantic resources, then Cixous is a genius of this genius. As Derrida puts it here, Cixous serves the French language 'in a manner both responsible and conscious of its inheritance, and nonetheless violent, unpredictable, irruptive, heteronomous, transgressive, cutting' (p. 22). Cixous is a genius of genius but perhaps both an evil genius whose genius undoes all the accepted and formal codes of a sovereign language as well as the good genie whose magical use of words opens new horizons, stretching the language in excess of itself. For to read Cixous is to read without model or map, neither critical, theoretical, or by literary precedent. This is what is perhaps most threatening to power about Cixous. The Cixous hyper-text which Derrida's essay salutes (this is the text of a lecture given at the inauguration of the Cixous archive at the BNF, the Bibliothèque Nationale de France) is unmasterable. Like other great literary inventors [*géniaux*] such as Homer, Shakespeare and Joyce, says Derrida, the Cixous oeuvre 'is potentially incommensurable with any library supposed to house them, classify them, shelve them. Bigger and stronger than the libraries that act as if they have the capacity to hold them, if only virtually, they derange all the archival and indexing spaces by the disproportion of the potentially infinite memory they condense according to the processes of undecidable writing for which as yet no complete formalisation exists' (p. 15).

The donation of the Cixous archive to the BNF is a dangerous gift because it compels the library to avow what it cannot comprehend, to guard what it cannot have, to house what it cannot master. Rather, the donation of Cixous's letters, notebooks and, above all for Derrida, her dream journals (for which every connection and no connection can be made with Cixous's novels and plays, involving centuries of scholarly labour – this text by Derrida is in part a counter-signature to the book *Dream I Tell You* which is a collection of some of the thousands of dream texts donated by Cixous to the BNF) represents an abyssal opening beyond the eyes of the library. This gift is the donation of all the secrets of the Cixous archive, which remain absolute secrets just as they are shelved and numbered in the BNF. Cixous has given the library an unconscious. That is to say, she has handed over to the BNF an all-powerful, powerless other. As Derrida puts it, 'the corpus remains immeasurably vaster than the library supposed to hold it' (p. 72). At the same time this corpus is only literature, that powerless challenge to power, whose strength is in its very weakness as the event of submission to the non-strength/non-sense of the other. The archive says everything (philosophical, poetic, political) and says so publicly as an affront to the sovereign without being of the sovereign. It can do so because it is literature and the sovereign can roar with impotent rage but will never master or possess the Cixous text, just as that text gives away (without giving up) all its secrets before the very eyes of the sovereign. If the BNF is the guardian and archivist of everything that has been written in the French language then it now plays host to both the evil genius and the good genie of Cixous, whose diurnal writing forces the archive into what Derrida calls a delirium [dé-lire] and forgetting [oublire] of reading, an avowal of what cannot be avowed, a reading of the unavowed, hence of a reading without reading. The archival competence of the BNF and of the Cixous-scholar-to-come is powerless in the face of this otherness and its structure of the undecidable. The best hope of such readers is, as Derrida says, to 'only confirm, work towards and cooperate in rendering [that structure] even more effective' (p. 34).

Towards the end of this text Derrida offers a conjecture, in which he suggests that if the donation of the Cixous corpus to the BNF 'is to be meaningful, that is, if it is to have a future, [it] should be at the heart of an active research centre, of a new kind, open to scholars from all parts of the world' (p. 83). With the sad and untimely loss of Derrida shortly after writing this essay (the reader will forgive me if I have continued to write of him here in the present tense: I have tried otherwise but I just cannot help myself) surely this speculation takes on a new urgency. Not only because the Cixous archive requires the immediate and scrupulous attention of a scholarship without reserve but because it is forever affiliated with what we must now call the Derrida archive. What architecture can we imagine that would link the Cixous collection at the Bibliothèque Nationale to the Derrida archive at the University of California, Irvine and to any future deposit of Derrida letters and manuscripts? What form would such a research-centre-without-condition take? How might it auto-immunise itself against ex-appropriation and the sovereign? How might it stay open 24 hours a day, 7 days a week, 365 days a year, to accommodate all the researchers of the world linked by the thread of Cixous–Derrida? What would be the spaces, virtual or imagined, material and concrete, of such a Centre without centre? Immediately we are thrown into the enormous problematic of the archive and the other which Derrida so deftly details in this text on Cixous, but it is a very real issue that the readers of Cixous and Derrida will need to take on. It is an issue (*the* issue) that has been arriving for some time now. In this sense it will have been wholly predictable and does not constitute an event as such but it does require a concentration of all the problematics of deconstruction (presence, the proper, the *archon*, the unconscious, translation, responsibility, the law, the gift, the title, the institution, inheritance, hospitality, the other and so on) to think through. Who dare take on this task of thinking a Centre that could have no presence, no onto-theological basis for authority? This global Centre would be entirely, as Derrida says of the character Gregor in Cixous's novel *Manhattan*, of 'bibliontological essence' (p. 16). And yet, it could take place tomorrow as the future of the archive.

What would be the remit of such a Centre? Well, Derrida has answered that in this text on Cixous: 'In order to learn to learn how to read, which is indeed indispensable, like knowledge itself, and like endless teaching and research, one must first read, everything, and read it all again, and again, in other words, first throw oneself headlong into the text, without restraint. Into the text of the other, into its Ominpotence-otherness' (p. 53).

Martin McQuillan

Notes

1 Jacques Derrida, 'The Future of the Profession or the University without Condition (Thanks to the "Humanities" what *could take place tomorrow)*', in *Jacques Derrida and the Humanities: A Critical Reader*, ed. Tom Cohen (Cambridge: Cambridge University Press, 2001).
2 Jacques Derrida, 'The Future of the Profession', pp. 26–7.
3 Jacques Derrida, 'That Strange Institution called Literature', in *Acts of Literature*, ed. Derek Attridge (London and New York: Routledge, 1992).

Un génie, qu'est-ce que c'est?[1]
A genius, what's that?*
What of genius?

What of this common noun that claims to name that which is least common in the world? The noun 'genius', one supposes, names that which never yields anything to the generality of the nameable. Indeed the genius of the genius, if there is any, enjoins us to think how an absolute singularity subtracts itself from the community of the common, from the generality or the genericness of the genre and thus from the shareable. One may readily believe genius generous; impossible that it be general or generic. Some would say that it amounts to a one-person genre. But this is another way of saying that it surpasses all genre of generality or the genericity of all genre. Another way of indicating that

---

* The original text of this book was the transcript of the opening talk of the symposium, 'Hélène Cixous: Genèses Généalogies Genres', organised by Mireille Calle-Gruber and held in the Bibliothèque National de France (French National Library), 22–4 May 2003.

1

it exceeds all the laws of genre, of that which one calls genre in the arts, literary genres, for instance, or what one calls gender, sexual differences. Not to mention humankind in general, for each time that one allows oneself to say 'genius', one suspects that some super-human, inhuman, even monstrous force comes to exceed or overturn the order of species or the laws that govern genre.

Oh, certainly – *certes*[2] – before I attempt, in my way, much later, after a great many detours, to answer this question ('what's a genius?' or 'what of genius?'), I shall first turn it every which way, I shall convert it. Three or four times at least. No longer *what's* a genius? *What* then? *What* about genius? But *who* is *a* genius? *Who* then? Then, a second conversion, what is *genius*? Not *a* genius, but *genius*?

Then, after that, a third conversion, how now to dare, overthrowing the masculinity of a French definite article ('*le* génie'), to decline this noun in the feminine?

And lastly, instead of turning to the third person ('who is this {*tel(le)*}genius?'), masculine or feminine, I address myself, for reasons I shall not immediately divulge, in the second person, to the second person: 'Genius, who are you {*qui es tu*}?'[3] I am asking you this question, genius, hear, do you hear?

Certainly – certes – everything I shall say will be '*tu*'.

Here now, bent on honouring the here and now we

have the unique good fortune to share in this place, I am about, as they say lightly, to *deliver* {*tenir*}[4] a speech, to hold forth.

How rash of me[5] to presume to hold forth! How unconscious I am! This flow or discursive, cursive, furtive and fugitive striding along that is commonly called the course of a discourse – how could it ever let itself be held? Restrained? Contained? How to maintain a discourse in the here and now? How not to renounce from the outset, reining in this beast, holding forth? I shall, *certes*, be unwise enough not to renounce, in any case to feign not to want to renounce – and furthermore, holding to my project of holding forth, it appears that I am about to do what I can to make my speech contain an untenable word. This untenable word, that no one these days would still admit holding to, is the common noun of genius. Herein apostrophised in every genre (hey you, who are you) in the masculine, true, but first and foremost in the feminine.

This noun, 'genius', as we are all too conscious, makes us squirm. And so it has for a long time. One is often right to view it as an obscurantist abdication to genes, as it turns out, a concession to the genetics of the *ingenium* or, worse, a creationist innatism, in a word, in the language of another age, the dubious collusion of some sort of biologising naturalism and a theology based on ecstatic inspiration. An irresponsible

3

and docile inspiration, a drunken submission to automatic writing. The muses are never far off. In according the least legitimacy to the word 'genius' one is considered to sign one's resignation from all fields of knowledge, explications, interpretations, readings, decipherings – in particular in what one hastily calls the aesthetics of arts and letters, supposedly more propitious to creation. Such resigning is considered mystical, mysticoïd. One is said to be confessing to dumb adoration of the ineffability of that which, in the usual currency of the word 'genius', tends to link the gift to birth, the secret to the sacrifice. But let us not rush to decry all secrets. If 'mystical' in Greek always invokes some secret, we shall perhaps need to resort elsewhere for this word, *mystical*.

The geniusness of whom? Who is it? Who are *you*?

Though it always marks a birth, a conception and a creation, who would dare, at this point, to inflect the name or noun of genius towards the femininity of an origin of the world? Here is one word {*le génie*} in our national language that has not yet been admitted into the dictionary of the French National Academy or into our National Library in the feminine. Not even, another grammatical singularity, to refer to a single person, in the plural. We should say, perhaps, if pushed, of a single person, a man or a woman, that she is a genius {*un génie*}, or that she has genius {*du génie*}. Never would we say that *she* is or *she* has, in the plural, more than one kind of genius {*plus d'une génie*}. The historical, semantic and practical singularity of this noun is therefore such that we have always kept it for the masculine as well as the singular. One has never, to my knowledge, recognised, in the feminine, *the geniuses* of a woman.

The future of this word becomes therefore stranger than the singular fate of its past. If this future is bequeathed to us, we shall have to answer for it. This is the responsibility I would venture to address today. What is going to happen with genius, that of this word, even? By choosing to write it in my title, I play, you perhaps think, at letting you guess that I mean to slip a proper noun in under the common one; that is, the feminine first name and patronymic, Hélène Cixous, towards whom all of us today here now turn. More than one {*une, f.*} genius in one.

Certainly – *certes* – this warrants detours and justification.

For I believe that I am up to something other than play here. Play at what, besides, and with whom? First of all, one might think, I am playing with the absence of a word, the word 'genius', to be precise, in the line of substantives belonging to the same family in *g* (geneses, genealogies, genres) that Mireille Caille-Gruber has judiciously selected for the beautiful arms of the symposium I am honoured to have been invited to. No, not only have I noticed a prudent, understandable and doubtless well-founded silence, the lack, the lapse, I shan't say the slip {*lapsus*}, but rather the ellipsis which in its flagrant absence cuts, like a fault line, through the semantic landscape of an entire generation of vocables. *Geneses, genealogies, genres*, in the plural. All that was missing, also in the plural, was *geniuses*.

Much later, were I to propose something like a thesis, I should try to show in what way the concept of *genius*, if it is one, must extricate itself both from the usual meaning of the word and even from its membership, albeit evident and likely, in the homogeneous, homogenetic, genetic, generational and generic series (genesis, genealogy, genre). Extricate itself and even upset the order of things.

I have just evoked 'the line of words belonging to the same family in *g*', to draw your attention without further ado to a multi-directional phenomenon.[6] A sort of crossroads or a chorus, should we wish to exercise our Greek memories, from Oedipus to Antigone, from the Eumenides to Helen. Such a multi-voiced phenomenon must for centuries trouble the wakeful vigilance of readers, interpreters, philologists, cryptologists of all ilk, psychoanalysts, philosophers, dramatists, historians, archivists, lovers of literature who will bend, as they say, over these fathomless depths, the oeuvre and *hors l'oeuvre*, or extraneous matter, that Hélène Cixous generously bequeaths to the French National Library — generosity, there's another word from the same family in *g*, close to geneses, genealogies, genres — and to genius. Or rather, as I shall specify in a moment in order to remain close to this enigma, they will bend over the unfathomed papers Hélène Cixous bestows upon — or lends to — this no less generous and enigmatic institution called the French National Library. Will it indeed prove itself a generous act of giving and giving back? And if yes, or if no, in what way? And laying the donation, and its donor and donees open to what dangers, to what hazardous responsibilities is one of the many questions that await us, and to which my tentative responses will be anything save reassured and reassuring. Such questions ought to be prowling around the essence, the destiny, the vocation and the future of an institution as extraordinary as a French National Library, as well as around Hélène Cixous's archive (oeuvre and *hors l'oeuvre*) on the day of this contracting, with mutual confidence, of a binding engagement and a quasi-will-like alliance, which will be my sole topic this evening. And my sole theme, for I shall rule out any remarks that do not refer directly and legibly to what is taking place in this place, in the here-and-now, to the experience of the event with which we are all associated – and asked to reflect upon.

A multi-directional phenomenon, as I was saying, crossroads, chorus, mingling of voices.

It so happens, *in the first place*, that what is at stake, tied up in this family of words in *g* (geneses, genealogies, genres) is the drama of a family as well, a drama of origins, of birth and of the derivation and filiation[7] of a name. Here we find, as her readers are well aware, the powerful, constant, tight-knit, outgoing and introspective thread of Hélène Cixous's work, her most intriguing plot[8] radiating from row upon row of some fifty-five books and her tens of thousands of unedited pages, letters, dreams or documents of all kinds.

If the phenomenon folds in upon itself and folds itself again, and again, it is therefore also, *secondly*, as it happens[9] (and I venture to say elliptically that genius may always consist in a *so-happening*, in finding, discovering or inventing oneself, in a meeting up with oneself at every turn, not just finding oneself, but finding oneself on every occasion, here or there, in a quasi-fortuitous manner, instead of the other, like the other in the place of the other), it happens, then, that this same family of words – genesis, genre, genealogy, generosity; and genius, etc. – is two-fold. It reflects itself, this word family, it finds itself in itself, it twists and it turns to find itself in order to say something pre-cisely about the family, birth and filiation. This family of nouns therefore also names the family names.[10] It pays its respects to the heritage of the name: genesis, genre, genealogy, generosity – and genius.

It so happens, *thirdly*, that everything seems to come back to the literality of a letter. Everything seems con-tained in the letter *g* (pronounced *gé* in French, as in *génie, générosité* and *généalogie*, or as in the *jet* {from *jeter*, to throw} of a toss of the dice, for instance). In the manner of the *logos*, proverbially considered to be in the beginning of everything, the letter *g* puts in writing the absolute initial of a first name and proper noun. Like the first name of God, title of Hélène Cixous's first book, this first name-proper noun precedes, guards and keeps watch over every initiation to the work. A first name, which happens, in life as in the books, to be the name of Georges the father and Georges the son, certainly – *certes* – a first name as ale-atory as it is destined (as it happens), a *first name* one might say is interpreted, chanced, bet upon, put into play, put on stage and on the air like the chef-d'oeuvre of the oeuvre. A first name omnipresent in reality as in fiction. It is everywhere, ever helpful, inspires every-thing, gets mixed up in everything, keeps watch over everything, it even goes so far as to keep its eye on the unconscious dreams albeit without the malevolence of an evil genie. The presence of this good genie is not even overweening, it is as discrete as a shade, silhouette more than alive and other than dead, just what's needed to be the bearer of a name that haunts all the books but also lends itself without stint to a thousand and one metamorphoses, metempsychoses and anagrammatic metonymies, among which the fictional first name of Gregor in one of the most recent fictions, the fictitiously called autobiographical *Manhattan,* is but an example among many.

What does one read in the *prière d'insérer*[11] of this book published less than a year ago but which might have been the first, or even the one before that? First of all, like the earth quaking between the body of the literary corpus and the body of her protohistory, or her prehistory even, between the archivable and the archiarchivable of a pre-archivable, or even an unarchivable which itself hesitates between fiction and memory, the phantasm and so-called reality, a reality which doubts itself at the very moment of its recounting, so-called reality. For, if one trusts the date referred to, 1964, these events of a life supposed to be real to which the book is said to refer pre-date the publication of any book by Hélène Cixous. So that the same *prière d'insérer* of this book dated 2002, *Manhattan,* subtitled *Letters from Prehistory*, is right to announce that what happens in the book (namely the events recounted in the mode of literary fiction) is not only outside but previous to all literature, to any work of literature signed Hélène Cixous. This, in a way, is undeniable but shouldn't stop us asking questions. Are things so simple? The *prière d'insérer* states:

> Everything happens in the before-work, a prehistoric season when the characters crazy about the great dead authors already picture themselves become books in their dreams, volumes, stealing up on the 'Oeuvre' they dream of stealthy as wolves, foolish as . . .[*]

An hors-d'oeuvre, a sort of exergue, the *prière d'insérer* reminds us thus that the story of what really happens in the book 'happens in the before-work' – now there's a task and a great deal of pleasure in store for biographers and such archivists as are legitimately concerned, but for that very reason how very unconcerned with distinguishing between the work, the before-work and the outside-the-work {*hors-l'oeuvre*}, the out-of-bounds {*hors-la-loi*} of the oeuvre. The archive's trustees may find themselves, because of the archive's devious structure, dispossessed of all power and all authority over it. The archive won't let itself be

---

[*] Hélène Cixous, *Manhattan. Lettres de la préhistoire (Letters from Prehistory)* (Paris: Galilée, 2002), *prière d'insérer*, p. 3.

pushed around, it seems to resist, make matters difficult, foment a revolution against the very power to
which it feigns to hand itself over, to lend and even to
give itself.

But above all, we are forewarned by the foreword
itself: it reminds us that the great symphometonymy of
the first names in *g* will be found, at the outset, for a
primal scene, as this morning, in a library. In *the* Library.
With a capital L. This *Manhattan* Library finds itself
then written, erected, monumentalised, capital-letterised. It figures the allegory of the absolute Library, both
tomb and conservatory-monument, hail and farewell.
A salute *to* Literature and salutary *for* Literature, survival and afterlife of Literature, 'Omnipotence-other',
'All-mighty-other' { *Tout-puissance-autre* }[12] as Hélène
Cixous calls and defines it. 'Omnipotence-other', a
hyphenated expression that is written, like the Library,
with the capital letter of an abstract noun (Library,
Literature, the 'Omnipotence-other'), a capital letter,
thus also appropriate for the first names in *g*, for
example Gregor or Georges.

In the handful of lines that I am about to quote, three
words in *b* also find themselves magnified by a
capital letter: *Baleine, Bannissement, Bibliothèque* { Whale,
Banishment, Library}. Books of exegeses would be
needed to account for the role they play in *Manhattan*
and in all of Hélène Cixous's work. I renounce as to so

12

many other necessary commentaries with which I shall not encumber the space and time so graciously granted us by this great French National Library, as yet unsuspecting of the problems that await it with the corpus that it is pretending like the Whale to swallow and keep down:

Among all the Jonases in search of the Whale in whose belly to perform the rites of banishment in those days was found [she too, as you can hear, says 'was found' {'*se trouvait*'}, and the biblical character Jonas, as well as the name Jonas, belong to the Cixous family and oeuvre, to the genesis, the genealogy and to works in all genres by Hélène Cixous; Jonas is everywhere at home here as, a line above, a paragraph, which alluded to the preceding book, *Benjamin à Montaigne. Il ne faut pas le dire*, has just reminded us: '. . . the character in *Amerika* by Kafka, whom Benjamin Jonas, my grandmother's little brother, was a great chum of . . .'] one Gregor, the really fabulous and uninterpretable character of this attempt at a tale.

One day in 1964 in Manhattan, at the turn of a destiny young but already marked by the rehearsal of the death of loved ones always called Georges, between the young woman who loved literature more than anything in the world and the young man whose mind was a copy of the Library's most spellbinding works, the mortal Accident occurs.

This fateful primal scene, the 'evil eye' scene, occurs *in reality* (just as if it had been written by Edgar Poe) in Yale University's tombstone of a library. (*Prière d'insérer*, p. 2.)

I pause my quotation for a moment. This time it so happens that a particular library is the setting, it delimits an appropriate theatrical space in which the action occurs. A certain library, *certes*, will have given place, led to or provided the occasion.[13] Metonymy or allegory of the universal library, and therefore already greater than itself, a certain library finds itself, lends itself or gives itself, as place, to the event, to that which we are informed has occurred '*in reality*'. This library that provides a place and an occasion is neither a universal library nor a national library, merely one library among many − located for its part in America, in Connecticut, and named without a capital letter. Beyond a doubt the library at Yale is a great exception, and especially the Beinecke here evoked; I know well this renowned edifice whose walls of stone let in an inoffensive, natural light, from the sun, to illuminate the archives of so many of the greatest writers of the 'Omnipotence-other' of world Literature. In the mammalian chamber of this Beinecke library, the author tells us she read, in all the languages, three *Ulysses*, Homer's, Shakespeare's and Joyce's. Each of these *Ulysses*, every one of their brilliant {*géniaux*} inventors,

14

is potentially incommensurable with any library supposed to house them, classify them, shelve them. Bigger and stronger than the libraries that act as if they have the capacity to hold them, if only virtually, they derange all the archival and indexing spaces by the disproportion of the potentially infinite memory they condense according to the processes of undecidable writing for which as yet no complete formalisation exists. This is also true of Hélène Cixous's great oeuvre, and I shall even say later why, in my opinion, it is true of each of her books, or even of every single letter.

Irreplaceable as it is for what happened there, the narrator tells us, '*in reality*', this singular library, the Beinecke, is merely one example, but infinitely capacious, of the great allegorical Library. Such is the reading situation into which we are thrown: in a work of fiction, we are told, and asked to believe, bearing in mind, above all, the visible emphasis of the italics, that what happened there happened *in reality*. But, such is also the law of the Omnipotence-other, therefore of Literature, that we are never allowed to decide, in this case as in the case of literature's great works of fiction, those of Poe in particular, whether this '*in reality*' hides a further simulacrum. In spite of the italics that seem to want to challenge the fictional, or rend its veil, despite these characters who wear their italics like the masks of theatrical personages or a tragic chorus stepping forward to warn us – 'Hear ye, know ye, this happened *in reality*' – it remains impossible to decide whether this '*in reality*' is an immanence of the fiction, like an upping of the fictional stakes, a further effect of the inventiveness, or even of autobiographical fiction, or of the dream or of the phantasm, or whether, on the other hand, the fiction takes this tear in its fabric seriously, if only to lead us on and stitch up elsewhere, in a thousand guises, the reference to what in fact happened, to what really took place in this place, *in reality*. Once only, on such and such a date, one day in 1964. Doubt and undecidability thicken in the remainder of the *prière d'insérer*, and thus in the book as a whole, since Gregor is a creature of letters (and in due time we shall see of what letters his name is made), Gregor, this 'young man whose mind is a copy of the Library's most spellbinding works', this being or figure of a library, Gregor, who is also defined as the 'really fabulous [what does 'really fabulous' mean? Really made of speech, like any fable?] and uninterpretable character of this attempt at a tale', Gregor, this 'personage', I would say, of bibliontological essence, 'all but unbelievable' as will be said a little further on. ('This improvised, dazzling, inaccessible hero, this all but unbelievable Gregor. / One has no more eyes.[14] I no

16

longer distinguish truth from falsehood, simulacrum from reality. I believe what one doesn't believe . . .')

There, in this example of undecidability – which could be multiplied ad infinitum, in Cixous to a greater degree than elsewhere, as if this were her very own signature and one of the many secrets of her several geniuses – there where it is impossible for the reader to decide between the fictional, the invented, the dreamt event, the fantasised event (including the phantasm of the event, not to be neglected) and the event presented as 'real', there in this situation handed to the reader, but to the librarian and archivist as well, lies the very secret of what one usually designates by the name of literature. There perhaps (and *Là* {*There*} is another of her book titles, the thriftiest, in two letters like *Or*) might be the secret of what she herself calls by the name of 'Omnipotence-other' or *Tout-puissance-autre*. Greater than any library, capital-L-Literature[15] begins to resemble, in a manner neither fortuitous nor insignificant, what it is not, namely God the Almighty, the Most-High and Wholly-Other. Unless God issues from Literature, is the All-mighty tissue of Literature.[16] God, the Genesis of Literature: the double genitive is here, grammatically, literally, the law of laws. Double genitivity, there's the subtitle I'd have suggested for this symposium's title so as to join an implacable logico-grammatical necessity to the genesis, the genre – and the genius.

Italics thus keep *the reality* of what is said to have taken place *in reality* in suspense, in literature. The italics make us reflect upon, even bring into play, the very body of the question: What is reality? What is an event? What is a past event? And what does 'past' or 'come to pass' mean, etc.? So many uncertainties or aporias for whoever claims to set a library's contents in order, between the library and what's outside it, the book and the non-book, literature and its others, the archivable and the non-archivable.

Therein lies literature's secret, the infinite power to keep undecidable and thus forever sealed the secret of what it/she {*elle*} says, it, literature, or she, Cixous, or even that which it/she avows and which remains secret, even as in broad daylight she/it avows, unveils or claims to unveil it. The secret of literature is thus the secret itself. It is the secret place in which it establishes itself as the very possibility of the secret, the place it, literature as such, begins, the place of its genesis or of its genealogy, properly speaking. This is true of all literary genres; and as we are aware, Hélène Cixous has, among all her different sorts of genius, that of practising, without exception, every kind of literary writing, from the critical or theoretical essay to the novel, to the tale, to theatre in all its forms. We shan't even mention poetry, for poetry is her language's element, most general of all genres, at all times the generating force behind her work, whatever genre it may be in. Furthermore the genres do not add themselves one to another, with her, they are not juxtaposed. It would be easy to come up with a thousand examples to demonstrate that in her *ars poetica* each genre remains itself, at home, while generously offering hospitality to the other genre, to all sorts of others which come along to interfere, to haunt it or to take their host hostage, always according to the same topodynamics of the smallest being bigger than the biggest: not only is the theatre in the theatre ('the play's the thing . . .') but dramas get staged in the novels, the Book has the right to speak and turns in turn into more than one character, even the act or the scene of a play, the Tale is fleshed out, given a capital letter, in a prosopopoeic allegory, speaking up in the first person, etc. The graft, the hybridisation, the migration, the genetic mutation is multiplied and cancels out differences of genre and *gender*, the literary and sexual differences.

Here we are kept at a respectful distance, within the magnetic field, but forever at arm's length from what one must call the secret of literature, the secret of its 'Omnipotence-otherness', or the genius of its secret. Before defining in a more formally theoretical manner what I mean by secret, then by genius, before returning, after a lengthy detour, to *Manhattan's prière d'insérer*, let us glance at the event of a moment, viewed from a certain angle of a labyrinth, this time in the secret interior of *Manhattan*'s library, after its *prière d'insérer*. As far as the secret goes, I could, of course, equally well have re-read with you *L'Ange au secret* {*The Angel in Secret*} (1991), that is to say the secret angel[17] as well, the angel whose emblematic attribute is the secret, as the bow and arrow are the attributes of Eros, but also the guardian-angel-of-the-secret, the good genie of the secret or again the angel pledged to keep secret, or again, the angel kept in a secret place, kept in secret; furthermore, the angel is the letter-bearer, in which case what is at stake is the secret dispatch of secret correspondence. What can a library do with secret letters? We shall define libraries in general as places devoted to keeping the secret but insofar as they give it away. Giving a secret away may mean telling it, revealing it, publishing it, divulging it, as well as keeping it so deeply in the crypt of a memory that we forget it is there or even cease to understand and have access to it. In one sense a secret kept is always a secret lost. This is what happens in general in the places one calls library archives. In *Manhattan*, she – Hélène Cixous – says: 'I had lost the secret, if I ever had it, of telling, the secret, the thing, the lens' (p. 43), this lens of the primal scene of which we spoke earlier.

A brief foray into *Manhattan: Letters from Prehistory* will allow us perhaps to specify *three things* at least, *three causes* – which are so many *laws*.

1. On the one hand, this secret, *certes*, like genius, possesses a force, a power, a *dynamis* of its own, a dynasty even since, as in the bequest of an archive, we are talking about an inheritance. Furthermore the secret employs inflexible violence in its petition. Having force of law, this secret is always the power of someone. There would be no secret without a pledge to the other. Without swearing. As such, this other, this person, so-and-so, is the secret and insists on secret. Imperatively, supremely, even if the tyranny of this dynastic injunction takes the gentlest, most innocent and most liberal of forms. The secret, rather than something, rather than being some 'which' or other, is always a 'who', the becoming a 'who' of a *that/id* {*ça*} that is attached to the secret which he or she is bound to keep.

2. Next, this should allow us to demonstrate that such-and-such a secret always hangs by some thread {*fil*}, and more than one thread, by threads {*fils*}, or by the sons {*fils*}, to the genesis, the genealogy and the genre, namely to that which has force of law in the matter of filiation or in the family phylum.

21

3. Finally, this will allow us to demonstrate that the secret is not without an affinity for the sacred, with the very genesis of that which, in a sacrifice, effects the sacred, brings forth or gives birth to the sacred and the secret in a single act of birth. Indeed, in this or that passage, once again in italics, what one must absolutely not lose sight of is the Cixous idiom. I would describe it, this idiom of a signature, as a kind of gift for letting itself be caressed by a genius of the language that cannot get over its utter surprise at the touch that comes out of the blue to move it and that breaks with the genetic filiation it respects and cultivates and enriches even as it betrays it. This betrayal out of faithfulness interrupts with an event the genius of the language, an unconscious genius of the language, unaware it was capable of letting itself be thus regenerated by that which seems to grow out of or derive from it. I am here envisioning the French language as a genius – we often say the genius of the language to designate its grammatical, lexical or semantic treasure, the infinite potentiality of its own resources, and I shall come back to this figure – but here of a genius of the French language which is served, in a manner both responsible and conscious of its inheritance, and nonetheless violent, unpredictable, irruptive, heteronomous, transgressive, cutting, by a completely different kind of genius. This latter, for the first time, softly, violently,

tenderly, opens its eyes to what lies within it, the French language, I mean, as if in sleep or sleepwalking in the infinite dream of its unconscious, finding itself there or finding itself back there without ever yet having found itself there. Along with the signature of the Cixous idiom, in the passage I am about to read I shall emphasise a literal allusion to dreaming. To the law of dreams. In so doing I mean to anticipate *two motifs* to my mind unavoidable in the extraordinary problematics and thus the implacable law that Hélène Cixous brings to bear upon this national institution to which she makes the both blessed and dangerous gift of her archive.

A. *On the one hand*, immense and active, the dream's immeasurable invasion of the genesis of her public writing, hence of her literature. I know of no more impressive and admirable example in the world of this kind of complicity, Hélène Cixous's indefatigable and unique translation of the infinite world, of all possible worlds of the nocturnal dream, into the incomparable vigilance of one of the most calculating of diurnal writings. This dream part does not merely furnish material; it also opens up the abyssal rift of a question ever-fresh (what is a nocturnal dream {*rêve*}? A diurnal? What is waking {*réveil*}? What time does she wake? And is it daylight when she begins to write? Is she still dreaming when she notes her dreams? Does she then begin to interpret them and shape them into literature? What is a consciousness or vigilance at work in the writing? But also: what is the *dream's* vigilance, the *dream's* thought? Etc.).

B. *On the other hand*, I believe that Hélène Cixous means to leave all or a part of her dreams, countless notebooks which have served, over decades, to collect her dreams. All or a part but which part? Where will she draw the line? How will she disguise or censor them? I refer here to the dreams noted upon waking, tens of thousands of pages, some of which will be immediately accessible, others much later, other perhaps never or never bequeathed, and this will cause the BNF {Bibliothèque Nationale de France, French National Library}daunting and, I fear or hope, I'm not sure which, insoluble problems, at once hermeneutical, oneirocritical and deontological, technical and ethico-legal. The line here would be drawn between literature and the others, between literature, Omnipotence-other, and its others, and non-literature, between the material and the form, private and public, secret and not-secret, the decipherable and the undecipherable, decidable and undecidable. So many conceptual pairs which here dwell in a perpetual fog, worse than oppositions, conflict, oppressive hierarchy or repression. The BNF will pay the piper, but so will Hélène Cixous, she above all, though differently. Now the other of the

'Omnipotence-other' of literature is not only but also dreams.

Rêve {*dream*}, there's a vocable that finds itself joined in her work, via alliance or alloying, to the significance of syllables and values bigger and smaller than its own body, at once included and including, such as *réveil*, *événement, revenir, revenant* {*waking, event, to come back, revenant*}, and above all, *Eve*, the first woman and Hélène Cixous's mother. In the English language, which exerts a constant attraction upon the writings of a foremost interpreter of Joyce and so many others from Shakespeare to Virginia Woolf, in so many British, American and French universities, *eve* is also the hour of vigil, of watch-keeping, as in *evening*. We might also and *even* say that *evening* is the secret watching-over an act of writing, which gathers and shapes, dreams and reveals {*rêve et révèle*} this quasi-*equation*, this restless equating, this turbulent equalising, *evening*, that comes and goes between *rêve, Ève, événement, éveil* and *réveil* {*dream, Eve, event, wake, waking*}. When I take the liberty of declaring, as I have just done, what I believe to be true, namely that Hélène Cixous intends to leave all or part of her dream memoirs to the BNF, I do not exaggerate. For what, in fact, do we read in the opening of the book that she is about to publish, the one that comes after *Manhattan*, with the so very

25

ambiguous title, in her grammar, of *Rêve je te dis* {*Dream I Tell You*},* a title in which the dream is at once the name of what I tell, the dream that I apostrophise, announcing to it that I'm about to tell it, describe it, declare it, avow it (dream, I tell you, I tell you as dream) and, then again, the verb in the imperative of a command (dream, this is an order given to the other, addressed familiarly, go ahead, dream, I tell you)? What do we read at the start of a work that thus represents a more or less considered selection of fifty dreams? Well, *Forewarnings* (in the plural, in place and form of a fore-word or a *prière d'insérer*) anticipate the text and give an inkling of the impossible and unending task that awaits the library reader. For a thousand reasons, of which I shall mention only three or four, gathered here in a single paragraph.

First of all, that a choice has been made. The author announces that she won't be giving us *all* her dreams. So as to respect their secrets. Over and above the abstract and partial nature, over and above the artful-ness of the encoding, of the disguising and the self-censorship, this implies a putting-into-shape. Even if she leaves the first draft, the *premier jet* (remember the word '*jet*') untouched, this shaping nonetheless consti-

---

* Published by Éditions Galilée in 2003 and in English translation by Edinburgh University Press, along with the present volume.

tutes a first, literary and public elaboration. It would be a good idea to reconstitute its articulations: with the remaining, immense corpus of the other dreams, of course, but also with the bulk of the published work. Cixous herself has apparently classified these dreams according to their more or less readily understandable connection with a number of her works (for example, *Beethoven, Messie, Or, Osnabrück, Le jour où je n'étais pas là, Manhattan* are the titles or indexes of dreams thus grouped by date). But what sort of connection? Did these dreams induce some motif or figure in the published work? But in this case, though enthusiasts of the genetic study of the manuscripts may be tempted to consider them enticing raw material, they do not have the same status as a first draft. Nor do they constitute rough work with crossings-out in view of a final version. Nor are they proof in the process of correction, etc. As in the illustrious cases of Mallarmé, Proust or Joyce. 'Genetic' or 'generic' study comes to a dead end here – but a dead end to knowledge which must neither discourage nor authorise obscurantist resignation. We must grant these dreams another fate and different histories depending on whether they have been published or not, as decided, deliberately and duly, by the author. Are they even contemporaneous with the literary writing? Are they marginal material, deletions, oneiric texts induced and later interpreted by the author, or on the contrary are the dreams the inducers? And if so in what way and how, each time, each time in its own singular and infinitely overdetermined way? And what if it were all that at once, inextricably? A huge and daunting task for the centuries of readers to come. Of these extraordinary *Forewarnings* which, in a few pages, provide so much food for thought as regards the givens, the gift and the giving of these dreams, I shall retain here, for the reasons and according to the rules I have announced, but a single paragraph, so as to point out, in three steps, the genius of the secret and the genius of the letter, above all of the syllable *gé*, with which we shall never be done, however it is transcribed (the letter *g*, the whole word 'jet', the word fragment 'gé', as in *génie* or *généalogie* or *générique*; and when the word 'genre' turns up in the same paragraph, not far from 'genesis', the paragraph contains all the words of our title to know it by. It must be quoted as an epigraph. I'll do it).

After having confided her submissiveness to the law of dreams, after having described the scene of the morning's transcription, then the secrets that she in turn 'discovers', Cixous goes on to tell us what she won't be telling us; she declares to customs the secrets she will not be revealing to the customs agents of the curious, the librarians, the critics and general readers. A veteran Freudian, she tosses this challenge to interpretation, to let the dreams interpret themselves, into the faces of the customs agents, not revealing the hidden contents, not revealing the proper names of the goods she's smuggling in. She even publicly swears that, saying *what* she speaks of, she will not say of *whom*. A contagious homonymy stands guard over the secret pseudonyms and metonymies, and over a French language whose idiom could hardly be better protected against the bloodless transfusion of translation than by its untranslatable homonymy.

> *These secrets, in this volume, I don't give them away. I never will. They know too much.* [If we understand the grammar correctly, it is therefore the secrets, those others, that know, they are the subjects of the knowing: the secrets know, it is not she who keeps the secrets that keep her. As for her, she finds herself kept in secret, held to the secret by the secret.] *I respect their reserve, their twists and turns, I admire their disguises. They had to be well hidden to slip through the cracks in my walls when I wasn't in the least prepared to let them come. And then time passed. One day you can look the dead person's photo in the face. When one had just died my death, yours, jets of boiling tears kept me from seeing your faces. The months of tears are past.* (p. 2)

There's the incredible grammar of those last sentences, their divided meaning, first of all, multiplied by the untranslatable homonymy of *les mois* {the months}, but also *moi*, me, the self, and *les mois* {selves, egos}, for example (*egos* as numerous as weeks in a month), all of it therefore calling for more commentaries than any library could contain: my death, 'one had just' she says (but who, 'one'?) died it, transitively, died it in my place, and my death is, in apposition, yours (who, you?) and then up spurt the 'jets of tears' (why *jets*, why this unusual word? Tears flow, they don't toss themselves up, one doesn't fling them up like projections or pro-jectiles to block your view ('kept me from seeing your faces')). To whom is she speaking, with these months and me's, you {*tu*} and you {*vous*} so as to recount my death, yours, your death, and your faces; your death can be hers, that of the me who is speaking and who speaks to herself, the one spoken of from the other place of the dream or the death of the *you* {*tu*} who, further on, in the same paragraph will be dissected, we shall see, with all the resources of its untranslatable homonymy, that is, of these irreducibly French homonymies, whose language all dreams recall (*tu*, meaning *toi*, *t*, *u*, *tu*, that which is struck dumb with the silence of the verb *taire* and *se taire* {to hush, hush up}, *le tu* {the you, the silence} of the secret, *le tu* as the genius of the secret: genius *qui est tu* {who is you, who is silenced} etc. Just as months of tears have gone by, like a period of time and the multiplicity of I's or me's who are others, four weeks and just so many *egos*, so there is the *tu* who is you and knows to fall silent or impose silence concerning itself).

> *The months of tears are past. Now I can gaze at the photo of your face without flaring up, pitiless dream. I admire the tapestry of signifiers that give the mask its extravagant features. A whole night with Handel, and I never suspected that the stately accents are those of the* haine d'elle, *the hate of her! I admire Freud's extraordinary power, first and last cartographer of these strange continents, the Shakespeare of the Night: he saw the movements and cosmonautic calculations of the whole* genesis [my emphasis] *and anthropozoology of this world, its wiles and passions, subterfuges and stratagems, intrigues and plots, games of* gender [my emphasis], genre [my emphasis again] *and species.*
>
> *Dreams are theatres which put on the appearance of a play in order to slip other unavowable plays between the lines of the avowal scenes . . .* (pp. 2–3)

'Other unavowable plays'. In this way the theatre of the dream, the theatre of appearance, smuggles in that which is and remains unavowable, even as it is being avowed, in the form and according to the genre of the avowal, brings it in clandestinely, as contraband. Whereupon, the reader-spectator is taken aside, apostrophised, addressed as friend, recipient–participant in this scene of the unavowable, an unavowable that is encoded, stubbornly hushed up[18] and which remains unavowed even as the avowal is taking place with its authenticity being vouched for. But what else might one avow, I ask, if not the unavowable? The avowable, if it is avowable, you must agree, hardly needs to be avowed. Only the unavowable may be avowed, were such a thing possible. Whereas the unavowable, inasmuch as it is the only thing avowable, one must admit, the logic is irrefutable, remains forever unavowable. And even if it is avowed, even if it finds itself avowed, it remains unavowable, therefore unavowed. The secret is that one can never catch up with the unavowable, it's a vicious circle, and thus one never avows. Even and especially when one avows. If one imagines the addressee to be the other who finds him/herself keeper of the archives, in a National Library, for instance, that is, above and beyond, therefore, other guardians of that which has first been written in the French idiom, hence in the homonymy which encrypts everything, well then, the BNF has been asked to stand guard over texts about which it, the BNF, must avow the unavowable, avow that it reads the unavowable, thus the unavowed. Hence it reads without reading, which can't be done save in a certain delirium.[19] Or what Cixous terms 'oublire': forgetread. The BNF, infinite memory of unreading and of forgetreading. The BNF, or all it represents and here brings together in the way of infinite readership, infinitely to come, must therefore avow that it does not comprehend that which it comprehends. It must avow it does not see {*voir*}, therefore does not have {*avoir*} that which it sees and believes it has, that it does not regard that which it guards, that which it keeps safe – saving its unconscious. Save in its unconscious.

It is as if, in the familiar, *tu* form of address, Cixous were speaking to every single person a Library, above all national, universal because or in spite of being national, represents and more precisely to its unconscious. Never has anyone so well addressed a library's unconscious. In order to say that the secret it keeps is not secret merely because it itself cannot access it, or because this or that part of its contents is hidden, encrypted, forever hermetic, but also because the form of writing, the literature entrusted to it, is so structured as to seal off its secret and make it undecidable, less a matter of hidden contents all in all, than of a bifid structure which can keep in undecidable reserve the very thing it avows, shows, manifests, exhibits, endlessly displays. The BNF and the universal readership to come find themselves all the more powerless, incompetent in their very competence, however keen, respectable, perfectible it may be, faced with this writing whose secret structure of indecidability the closest, the most cultivated of readings can only confirm, work towards and cooperate in rendering even more effective.

The 'Forewarnings' to *Dream I Tell You* speak to us thus:

> *. . . you reader-spectator are aware of this but you forget what you know so you can be charmed and taken in. You connive in your own trickery. You pull the wool over your own eyes. The thinner than a razor blade that slips between you and yourself is an imperceptible vertical hyphen. You are a you* {Tu es un tu}. *Do you see what I mean? Who is* you? [It is because of this 'qui est tu?' that I began with the question 'genius, who are you?'] *I am reminding you of the dream's delicate work; first it slips the invisible laser scalpel between the letters: t, u, t'es eu, tu,* {you've been had} *next between the signifieds Siamese twinned by homonymy: tu es tu* {you are you} *that's why, étant tu* {being you/having remained silent} *tu ne peux plus te taire* {you can no longer remain silent}. *As for the bistouri* {scalpel}, *il bisse tout ris* {repeats, echoes, all laughter}.
>
> *I'd better stop: I don't want people to bristle at the thought of the philosophical and philosophicomical resources of the language.* (pp. 3–4)

And indeed she knows to stop on the brink of mere cleverness, when the signifier, being mere signifier, is no longer significant. But of the Siamese, untranslatable homonymy of *tu* which reduces you – you – to silence and secrecy, falling silent and being silenced, we know we know nothing: who is the *tu/you* to whom she says '*tu est tu*', you are, as English puts it, *silenced*. You shall not speak and you won't be spoken of, I promise you, you promise me, I promise myself, *tu sera tu*, you yourself and no one else. The law is yours, it is yours and only yours, it is reserved, destined for you, *nur für dich bestimmt*, as it is said of the man 'before the law' in Kafka. As for that which might, here or there in the 'Forewarnings', seem excessively playful and artificial, for example, the 'bisse tout ris', you must wait to see the dream of 9 January 1995 for the scene with Fatima (the dedicatee of the book, she whom in real life has transcribed the dream manuscripts along with so many other texts, and deserves universal gratitude for what these writings said to be transcriptions imply, namely, not just knowledge, conscientiousness and patience, but a way so subtle, so intelligent of being in tune with the texts). The scene in question is a genesis, a hospital delivery involving Eve, the mother-midwife in real life, whom the dreamer orders to 'take her bistouri', while Thessa (alias Thessie) bites down on a cushion on which one sees a mysterious tiger, strangely nicknamed 'petigre' {litiger} – who might this be, one wonders – and who seems to know more than it lets

35

on, a tiger painted on the pillow, substitute for a lost kitten, etc.

Now, after all these precautions, here is the passage I spoke of, at the heart of *Manhattan* this time, quoted from *Manhattan*, as is proper. Wholly slanted towards the italic, as a quotation or a transcription upon waking from a dream might be. This long paragraph thus seems to originate in a dream – and associates the secret with the sacred, just as, to the crying out of the sacrifice,[20] it allies the 'force of the Secret'. The Secret of this force, the secret that is a force, the force that is a secret: there you have so many possible definitions of all kinds, all genre of genius. This Secret is capital-letterised in the text, and all but personified. The force of such a Secret is not something, it is not a substance, an impersonal or a natural energy, once again it is someone. The capital letter sets the scene for prosopopeia. Not of a mask or talking face but of someone who, knowing how to keep silence, and being silenced/being you {*être tu*}, a *tu*/you pledged to the silence of the unavowable, knows how to {*s'entend à*}[21] keep a secret or, from its Omnipotence-otherness, to impose the categorical imperative of absolute secrecy, if tacitly, without saying a word:

Monday 2 April 2001 [the passage in italics thus opens with a date which interrupts the calendar of the tale told,

36

that is, what is supposed to have happened *in reality* in 1964, so as to come back to the present, the here and now of the tale telling itself or of the writing writing itself], *antipathy for the word Sacrifice woke me* [she was asleep, she has therefore just wakened, been awakened, at dawn, by the word Sacrifice which also, like the Secret, like the earlier 'force of the Secret', is allegorised with a capital letter], *the word sacrifice turns up every morning, it's the first one on the paper at seven* [therefore the sacrifice or rather, to spell it out, the noun 'sacrifice' is every morning, at seven, first up, the first one awake and to wake, in the life of the author. That which then awakens and wakes, is the start of a word, 'sacrifice', the substantive 'sacrifice' in a word, even, you shall see, in more than a word, the vocable 'sacrifice' undergoing fission, splitting up into the sons and crying out of filiation], *it's a fiesta in the living world, birds warbling their celebration joining the chorus one after another and signing their presence in the notebook of the world with a note or two on this day, a model of respect and joy which we, non-birds, restless humans, haven't the nervous systems to imitate at seven a.m. in the notebook of the world peace is signed by the birds, but the word Sacrifice bounces off my pen, sticky with blood crawling with vermin.* [Hence you would think the word Sacrifice *throws itself* {*se jette*} under her pen as if under an automobile to kill itself and find itself in shreds, as you will see, in a sort of self-sacrificing suicide-attack that will cut

37

the sacrifice itself to ribbons, the word sacrifice, breaking it down or disjointing it, not so as to disjoint the language but, on the contrary, in order to reconstitute its scattered limbs, in an exclamation.] *By dint of listening to it scrape its funereal wings across my flint, I hear it, and I note its notes. Ah! it cries: son!* { *Ça crie: fils! / Sacrifice!* } *You took your time I tell myself.* [The sons cry out everywhere in Cixous's work, the son cries out or is mute, *infans*, their census would never end. To mention only the two previous works, I refer you to the brother called '*fils fui*', 'fled son', at the end of *Benjamin à Montaigne*,[*] and above all to *Le jour où je n'étais pas là* { *The Day I Wasn't There* }, whose lost son is not perhaps without a connection at least chronologically – I make this encrypted suggestion to the archivists – to the Gregor of the library.] *And I bowed to the impressive Forces* [capital F] *that govern us: the force of deafness, voluntary, the force of refusal, involuntary, the force of flight, involuntary, and the force of the Secret* [capital S] *which is patience without end, total resistance to time. No way to dislodge it. It plays dead. But it's a false dead: no decomposition. It lives outside us within us dies without deteriorating for decades. Immobile, it directs the whole of our play and we know nothing of it. It is the reason for all our choices and our non-choices, cause of our follies, author of our errors and of our discoveries.* (pp. 29–30)

---

[*] *Benjamin à Montaigne. Il ne faut pas le dire* (Paris: Galilée, 2001), p. 249.

Hence she is writing, it must be said, upon waking. She is writing, certainly – *certes* – *upon waking* {*au réveil*}, what must we read between the lines of these words? That she writes at the moment of waking, of course, as we have just been told ('*antipathy for the word Sacrifice woke me, the word sacrifice turns up every morning*'); she writes upon waking, at dawn, she writes *on* waking, with the help of waking,[22] as they say, and it's true, she writes by hand, on the edge of the bed when she writes down her dreams. She always writes by hand, no matter what, she writes using a tool – pencil or pen – that is, without a machine or a machine-tool; without a typewriter or a word processor. Something which is fairly unusual and of critical importance for the immense archives of which we speak, and I should have liked to have devoted some remarks, among all those the occasion demands, to Hélène Cixous's phenomenal handwriting, to its form, to its lines, to its rhythm and to the economy of its quasi-stenographic shorthand, to its graphic body and to the archival stakes in all that. Whoever has not set eyes on the lines of her handwriting will be missing something essential of the vivacity and animality they communicate to the body of the published text, the supple handling of the pen, the patient acceleration of the letter: fine, lively, agile, sure, economical, clear, legible running on in an uninterrupted and unimaginably curious cursiveness, careful that is, to find quickly, not to lose an instant and not to let itself be overtaken by what she finds herself finding even before she has looked for it, even if we know she has been looking for it for centuries and has always known where she has looked for what she has just found at the very spot, in the crook of this branch. Her handwriting reminds me of all the squirrels in the world.

Thus from the start she writes on waking, by hand, on the edge of the bed, on one of the thousand or ten thousand notebooks the BNF is to inherit. She writes upon waking in order to write down her dreams. But often, as in the paragraph we have just read, the dream itself comes along to interrupt sleep. The dream wakes up.[23] The dream keeps watch, inflexible, ever ready to summon up the wakefulness, the consciousness ever vigilant in the memory of the dream – and what an incredible memory! I know of none to match it. The dream then gives the order to write down, to note, even to begin to analyse it, the dream. Which keeps its force and its initiative and its secret, even as it uses unstintingly of the power it has over her, over the writing that bends its willing body to it. 'She writes on waking', so this must be understood not only as 'she writes at the moment of waking', but also just as 'she writes in pencil, in ink, by hand', she writes fuelled by the oneiric energy of the dream, as one would say of a

40

missile that it is propelled, for example, and driven by atomic energy. Her writing is set in motion by waking, at the moment of waking but also, thanks to the energy of waking, she works on waking, she burns the energy of a waking which is the order of the dream as well, *at* the order of the dream but not *of* the order of the dream, at the order of the dream which also orders, actively and passively, its own interruption. The dream switches itself off. How can this be? It falls silent while giving itself to be spoken of, in its place. It falls silent/it is you: *il est tu*. But the waking, this first waking is already on the lookout, it keeps watch with all its might, it keeps watch without stint, it supervises, still it keeps vigil over the dream, it dreams of rousing all the powers of the interrupted dream. Of the dream that has just fallen silent, for it has just fallen silent/it comes to fall silent {*il vient de se taire*}, it comes from that which it silences even as it speaks. Waking is poised on the edge of the silent dream, as if the dream that had passed might still be coming or coming back. (An occasion to touch, too rapidly, in passing, upon the unfathomable enigma of a sort of disaffiliation, in the great language of France, between two word families one might have thought related. I refer to a surprising etymological dissociation between the nouns *rêve* *(rêverie, rêvasserie)* or the verb *rêver,* on the one hand, apparently of unknown origin, pure French, lacking cousins in any other language, and, on the other hand, the vigilance of the vigil, of *veille, éveil, réveil*, lexical items whose Latin affiliation is rich and evident. Between *rêve* and *réveil*, in sum, no relation, no family tie, as is proper and as if the latter, the *réveil*, had nothing to do with the former, the *rêve*.) To write on waking is to devote oneself body and soul, every single morning, to a scene of resurrection and adoration. A prayer on the edge of the bed, prayerful words lovingly addressed, like a letter written on the body of the dream, to the dream body, but also inscribed upon the very body of a dream now awakened, if not answered. But also an utterance written *to waking*, addressed to and intended for waking. As if the waking, coming out of the dream, following in the grieving footsteps of the dream, in its *wake*, were still listening for the dream. For a dream already dreamed which yet waits to be dreamed again, wakened and shown to itself, verily.

As if subject to the authority of a verdict whose *veridictum*, whose truth insists on being told, the dream by itself brings itself to an end, while keeping itself: both intact and transfigured, sometimes encrypted in its transcription. Scribbled in haste, but carefully, with the help of a system of abbreviations and initials more cursive than ever, all these notes of dreams survive, transitively no doubt, the colour, the emotional intensity and the trace of this event both extraordinary and daily, which consists, for the time of the dream, in interrupting itself, hardly catching its breath, every morning very early (for a long time she has gone to bed early and so risen early, as if to cultivate this alchemistry of the dream and bring to light this upwelling of writing upon waking). In interrupting itself, the dream keeps the trace of this interruption upon waking as well as a trace of that which may thus have been cut off. Tens of thousands of dreams noted down will require centuries of deciphering – notably in the tangle of threads that ties them to the work published and called literature, fictional, theatrical, didactic even (for Hélène Cixous's academic work, also creative, like her research and teaching, despite its own, specific, particular, disciplined demands, leaves a monumental archive of its own, on various supports – paper notes, audio- and videotapes – which, I would say, are always essentially in complicity with the rest of the corpus – literary, fictional, public or not, including the unincluded, the incomprehensible corpus of the dreams). But to write on waking implies something else yet again. A hymn addressed to waking, perhaps, but especially, what is something else entirely, and a completely other waking, the writing on waking marks an absolutely heterogeneous break. One can, if one likes, call this literary conscience. But it is a more conscious conscience, whose heterogeneity consists also in being in a situation of heteronomous obedience to the Omnipotence-other of literature. Now the caesura of this other waking does not fall between the time of the dream and the first moments of waking, but leaps in to make an interruption in the interruption that sets in motion the work of the vigilant writing, the diurnal time of the literary act proper. This, while miraculously keeping the thread of the dream going (this, for me, is the miracle), the gift of the writing, nonetheless cuts it off instantly and knowingly transfigures all the givens, taking into account, so as to incorporate as well as surpass them, all the resources of a vast literary experience, an incomparable science of the language, of the thousand and one libraries of universal literature so as to create events totally without precedent, and without imitators, no schools possible, there where, as I shall show in a moment, the genius consists precisely in making the work come, giving it room, giving, period, giving birth to it as event, paradoxically breaking with all genealogy, genesis and genre. This is where, as I shall explain more fully in a moment, the genius-ness of all genre of geniuses is no longer part of the homogeneous family of genesis, genre and genealogy. One could find an example of this rupture, within the fiction itself, in *Manhattan*, once more, when, following the passage transcribed in italics, on Monday, 2 April 2001 (on the subject of the word *sacrifice* and the 'force of the

Secret'), she continues, in roman type: 'The evening of Certes I noted', etc., words followed, as at the very beginning of the book and first chapter entitled 'Certes a Sacrifice', by an impressive piece of work on the words *côte, à côté* or *aux côtés de* {*coast, hill, rib . . . beside . . . at the side of, alongside . . .*} her brother. The book opens with a sentence that ought, like so many others, to be remembered for eternity: 'I didn't want to go to Certes and there I was on my way side by side with my brother I'm forever doing what I didn't want to do I was thinking . . .' The toponym Certes, in its adverbial form 'certes' {*certainly, truly, to be sure*}, once again capital-letterised, is the anagram or cryptonym of *Secret*. In the title 'Certes a Sacrifice', one cannot tell whether the capital letter marks the first letter of the phrase or a proper noun. Afterwards, one can understand, provided one is not too dozy, that Certes, capital C, is one of the innumerable crypts, the turning-into-a-proper noun of an adverb. Certes is the Secret, the anagrammatic transformation of Secret. Certes is the trope or the Secret place of the story that you will never reach. Certes, as place, is one of the most fantastic personages, which is to say, in the rhetorical sense, as figure or trope, and as secret destination – or secret destinee – the somebody who keeps the force Secret, its anagram. Unless it is the force of the secret that keeps her. Each time I have said *'certes'*, and you may have noticed that this has been often, secretly I was murmuring *secret*, the reverse of a well-kept secret.

This waking within the waking is therefore the extreme vigilance of a most refined and practised literary conscience, a most audacious one as well, but also a highly supervised and supervising one, one skilled like none other at founding itself on literature's secret, that is, on the cryptopoetic power that seals up everything, sign and seal of universal literature in new French language, everything one must not tell. She seals off, she blocks, blocks as one boards up a door or as one sentences the reader not to read what he reads or condemns[24] him to read what he doesn't know how to read. To stand before the boarded-up door, while he strolls in the endless labyrinth as if the door stood ajar. Everything that Hélène Cixous gives to the BNF will remain sealed, readable unreadable, that is, marked with the sign or verdict of this boarding up which not only has never kept anyone from reading, but opens on the contrary an infinite field to reading and its pleasures – to the love of the Omnipotence-other of Literature. The door is barred but please come in. Make up your own mind. I recall the subtitle of *Benjamin à Montaigne*: *you mustn't tell*, and the subtitle, in parentheses, of the most powerful play I have ever seen, *The Story (you will never know)*.

Is what separates genius, then, from everything that might seamlessly connect it to a genesis, a genealogy or a genre, not this absolute event that marks the unde-cidable limit between the secret and the phenomenon of the secret, between the absolute secret and the phenomenal appearing of the secret as such? This is where the genius of inspired events plays along with Literature, with its Omnipotence-other. For Literature draws this undecidable line the instant it whips the secret it keeps from you into its cipher, out of sight, true, but that it keeps {*garde*} absolutely while handing it to you to look at again {*re-garder*}, but without holding out any hope of your grasping it, that is, while depriving you of the power or the right to choose between reality and fiction, between fiction which is always a real event, like the phantasm, and so-called reality, which may always be nothing but a hyperbole of the fiction. That, at least, is how I interpret the word 'other' in the term that Cixous reserves for Literature, 'Omnipotence-other' { *'Tout-puissance-autre'*}. I shall not insist, having done so at length elsewhere, on what she does with the word 'puissance' in the French lan-guage. I should, however, like to attempt to explain the other, the attribute 'other', in the expression 'Omnipotence-other'. This omnipotence {*puissance*} peculiar to literature consists in giving you (it is a gift, of genius, and generous), in giving you to read at the same time it prevents you {from reading}, or rather thanks to the power {*pouvoir*}, thanks to the grace granted you to withdraw or to deny yourself the power and the right of deciding, of choosing, between reality and fiction, personal testimony and invention, between what really happened and phantasm, between the phantasm of the event and the event of the phantasm, etc. This omnipotence {*puissance*} that governs you gives you the power and takes it back again, it gives you the power and the right to read while refusing you any position of authority, making you yield to it. It is therefore, properly speaking, a heteronymous kind of omnipotence. It is a law that we do not give ourselves in any autonomous manner. It delivers us over to the experience of the wholly-other as might {*puissance*} of the wholly-other or Omnipotence-other. But literature, forsworn heir in this to the Holy Writs, heir both more than faithful and unpardonably blasphemous of all the Bibles, remains the absolute place of the secret of this heteronomy, of the secret as experience of the law that comes from the other, of the law whose giver is none other than the coming of the other, in this test of unconditional hospitality which opens us to it before any condition, any rule, any norm, any concept, any genre, any generic and genealogical belonging. The unconditional hospitality of this singular gift exposes us and disposes of us before we so much as dream of proposing, inviting or awaiting any predetermined being whatsoever.

I say 'exposes us', I ought to specify 'throws us' {*nous y jette*}, for this is an expression that recurs frequently (as earlier talking about the 'word sacrifice that throws itself', but we could find a thousand other examples). What is the thrownness of what *throws us*, and that, by definition, is more mighty than we are – mightier than us in us? This thrownness resembles both the movement or the flutter of a pulse, an urge, a compulsive and irresistible impulse that cannot not go, as if self-propelled, to face the most dangerous wholly other, but which gives itself also, pledges itself, throws itself like a river into the sea, like a vulnerable, abandoned child, into the test of dereliction (*Geworfenheit*) where the -*ject*, the being-thrown of that which throws itself while finding itself thrown precedes all subject, all project, all object, all objection or all abjection. And this precisely because the *jet* of *se jeter* {to throw oneself} is at the mercy of the other, of the Omnipotence-other, called by the other, caught up by the other before any reflexivity, were it suicidal. When one throws oneself on the other, whether from love or for murder, one always comes up on the jetty, the other's thrownness, which finds itself thrown there ahead of one.

But the syllable '*jet*', before being embedded, or snipped from a word, this syllable '*jet*' whose many resources both Latin and philosophical (subject, object, project, ob-jection and ab-jection, one could add *sub-jectile*) I have just mined in order to make them communicate underground with the name of the father in *g*, as well as with a German idiom also present in the Cixous genealogy through her German-speaking mother, thus with the Heideggerian thought of being-thrown as *Geworfenheit*, but also with the translation of *Gegenstand*, of this object that one also used to call, before Kant, *Gegenwurf* (what is thrown in front, ahead of, counter to), and thus of all that runs counter to or encounters in the poetical-semantic chain whose thought Celan adjusts and reconfigures in *The Meridian* (*gegen*, counter, *Gegend*, the region, *Gegenwort*, the counter-word of Büchner's Lucile, the *Gegenwart*, the here-and-now, and *Begegnung*, the encounter); we must grant that this extraordinary three-letter syllable in *jet* has at least two semantic fields {*portées*}[25] (in the sense of the musical stave, of period of gestation and of litter or brood) or, equally, two extraordinary destinies.

On the one hand, it covers and stirs up the whole history of that which, in thought, philosophical thought or the thought of philosophy in particular, such as it seems to me, in its most original developments, brought into play in this work, finds itself pre-configured by the figure of the *jet* (object, subject, project, objection, abjection, *Gegenwurf*, *Entwurf*, *Geworfenheit*), and by the figure of *jeter-lancer* {throw-toss} in the toss, the uncertain toss of the dice, namely, the idea of the event, of the arrivingness of whatever or whoever arrives, of the other as that which happens, an idea forever indissociable from the experience in the course of which the dice are tossed.

But, *on the other hand*, this powerful formalising of the *'jet'*, which encompasses the greatest generality of the Cixous library, which forms her element in the sense of general 'milieu', is also strewn about like an atomic particle, an all but insignificant phoneme or grapheme, as element, here in the sense of the atomists' *stoikheion*, in the sense of the letter or of the minimal composition of letters in the syllable, word or word fragment. Like a strewing {*jetée*} of words for example, and I shall limit my clues to a certain dream of 25 March 1997, from *Dream I Tell You*. Without mapping all possible routes through this very dense page, I shall favour the red line of a fire, the fire of an ardent love which enflames the whole dream and whose fire, one might say, catches the word, from the letter to the syllable, then to the vocable, *jet, jeter, je t'adore, jet'* {*I adore you I adore you Iad I you*}. Here are some fragments of this dream:

In this huge fair, big as city sprung up for a day, everything keeps us apart and everything unites us. The miracle, or our luck, is that despite everything we manage to meet and *toss off* fiery words. [. . .] That's how amid the great crowds of the fair, carried away by love's fever I find myself next to you in a packed metro train [. . .]. At the stop, suddenly, your voice close to me, as if it were my own, calling soundlessly, in my very being, I adore you I adore you I adore you. In the noise of machines and people the words are softly shouted, a little anxious, it is God's gift and as the automatic doors eject me I shout me too because what else can I say. Then *fired up* and hurrying, I retrace my steps to my room where I must prepare to meet you again in public later. [. . .] I've been spared nothing. But still that night I managed to join you. And your *ardent* words are in my life, I adore you I adore you Iad I you {*je t'adore je t'adore jeta jet'*} (pp. 120–2: my italics)

One does not know, *certes*, whether these words or syllables are her words or the other person's, the other's in that they are uttered by the other or the other's in that they are addressed to the other, to the you ('And your ardent words are in my life, I adore you I adore you Iad / *Et tes mots ardents sont dans ma vie, je t'adore jeta jet"*). These febrile words, these fiery or feverish words which little by little dwindle to nothing, like a burning paper whose ashes only let us read, in the end, last breathless archive, blown out on the caught breath of an expiration or a last sigh but also an apostrophe, the three-letter syllable 'jet' – followed, precisely, by an apostrophe left dangling, I adore you {*je t'adore jeta jet'*}, cut off only to be repeated breathlessly. A sigh is withheld when, as was stated in the first sentence, 'despite everything we . . . toss off fiery words'. This '*jet*' (that one can only read, for it is unpronounceable, between '*jet"* and '*je t"*) is not only the *jet* or the genius of the writing; it is the double element of the corpus, its element as a theory of sets, *set theory* or *jet theory*, but also an atomic element, a sort of genetic cell or link in the chain of DNA, one of the smallest possible writing particles, but also a litiger capable of biting on everything, of swallowing the whole, a smaller bigger than the biggest.

Whoever might want to tackle the taxonomy and indexing of such a paradoxical body of work would have also to consign or countersign the whole of the French language, all the *g*'s and *j*'s of the French language. Hence admit the inadmissible: the task is beyond the limits of our knowledge. In order to learn to learn how to read, which is indeed indispensable, like knowledge itself, and like endless teaching and research, one must first read, everything, and read it all again, and again, in other words, first throw oneself headlong into the text, without restraint. Into the text of the other, into its Omnipotence-otherness. Learning to learn

how to read, how to read her, I don't believe has happened yet, save in some rare instances. There is, *certes*,
an undeniable celebrity quality, Hélène Cixous's aura
and global reputation. But strangely, these go along
with a lack of appreciation, in France above all. This
state of affairs deserves lengthy, discriminating analyses.
These would, needless to say, first of all take into
account the writing or the poetics, they would study
the language whose untranslatability, although rooted
in the French idiom, for that very reason, paradoxical
as it may seem, resists the codes and customary usages
of French language and literature. It resists them, one
might as well say it encounters fierce, frightened,
threatened, denied resistance. The same analyses
should show how these resistances are tied to those of
the people and powers-that-be of French culture, its
university, its schools, above all its media. What Hélène
Cixous's work does to these codes is a storm so unpredictable and so intolerable that there is no question of
her garnering a following. The dearth of readers
formed by or to this work makes the clear-sighted,
insightful and premonitory hospitality that the BNF
grants her here today all the more significant. We must
pay extraordinary homage to this institution. We must
acknowledge it as the prestigious and sole depository of
copyrighted publications, certainly – *certes* – and of hal-
lowed archives. But this keeper of the past's noble her-

itage is also, as it happens, because of its very tradition-
ality, the bold and prophetic fore-keeper, I dare say, of
masterpieces to which, despite all the resistances I have
noted, a future is promised. Such a fore-keeper is vital
for the Omnipotence-other of literature, inasmuch as,
without being nationalistic, this literature, in this
country, is linked in its events to the body of the language called French whose life and survival it ensures:
a time-to-come in a word. I am sure I speak for all of
Hélène Cixous's admirers when I express my gratitude
to the BNF, but gratitude is due, above all, needless to
say, to Marie-Odile Germain. Better than anyone, in all
its minutiae, she knows the interminable and daunting
task she assumes with such generosity, devotion and
time-tried competence.

That which I shall try to approach as I attempt to
redefine genius is not unrelated to this heteronomy
that delivers us, in literature, over to what Hélène
Cixous calls the 'Omnipotence-other'. The hyphen
between these two words seems destined to indicate
that these three significations, the absolute, the powerful and the alterity, are basically one and the same
thing, the same Cause (*Ursache,* as she often specifies),
and the same law – as literature. We would be wrong
to think that this experience of genius is merely a
matter of obedient and passive reading; it tries the
endurance that throws us into the writing. And if this

word *omnipotence,* the omnipotence-other of literature, is linked, by the same link, to that which I shall little by little, but wholly otherwise, define as genius, the genius of literature or the geniuses of Hélène Cixous, this is because *puissance* is a word that has only recently entered the old new French language via an operation I have elsewhere described, showing how Hélène Cixous took its grammar by force, from an incredible use of the present subjunctive {*puisse*} and the quasi-present-participle '*puissant*' which suddenly appears to start to slip and slide, *to derive,* a demonstration I must bank on but that I do not wish to reproduce here. I must leave it too aside, as I must leave everything aside that, in this demonstration, cannot be separated from the paradoxical lexicon, logic and topology of *côte* and *côté* {*coast, slope, rib, side, beside* . . .} in Cixous's work.

That this Omnipotence-other deprives us, in the name of literature, of the right or the power to choose between literature and non-literature, between fiction and documentary, is a new state of affairs in the world and in the history of humanity. The consequences and implications are mind-boggling. Not just in the realm of law (for even the genesis of the law is at stake here). The situation's givens are unfathomable and fascinating for a great national Library to which are entrusted, like so many challenges, archives whose status as literature we are hard put to decide upon, whether that which is legitimately classified, and legally copyrighted in the category of 'literature', does or does not shelter reliable references to what occurred 'in reality', an object therefore for historians or biographers; or whether it even tallies, thanks to a homonymy ever ready to trick us, with realities indexed as such in documents of a testimonial or testamentary nature. The librarian will always find it difficult to decide if the referent of such and such a text and document is real or fictional, or in the case of the texts of dreams, even more undecided between reality and fiction, unemployed materials, if I may say, or materials not yet literary with an eye to literature, available for literature, explicitly or implicitly destined to be put to literary work, therefore *already* literary though *not yet* literary etc. Those who, here in this room or among her friends, readers or admirers, are already familiar with the Cixous archive know to what degree in her case especially, more than elsewhere, such problems are and will become increasingly crucial, forever insoluble perhaps, thus at the heart of indecidability, cooperating in a decisive manner with the problematisation, elaboration, transformation and renewal of all these questions. These are *practical* questions, *certes*, practical first of all in the *technical* sense of the term (classification, dating, categorising, cataloguing, delimiting the internal boundaries of the corpus), but also *practical* questions in the *ethical* or *deontological* sense of the term (what has one the right to classify as literary fiction or as non-literary document? Who authorises whom to unveil what of the secret or of the non-secret in a public work of literature? Who authorises whom and authorises himself what in order to permit the divulging of such and such identifiable filiations or relationships in the genesis of the work employing private non-literary documents (dreams and letters, for instance) it has been legally decided will never or not for decades enter the public domain, etc.?).

This is why I had to cut short my first quotation at the word 'library', at the words 'tombstone of a library'. These words allow us to conjure up an all but mute institution, dedicated to the deathly silence of a tomb closed up over its genius, that is, over life (for genius, as its name indicates, always bears witness *for life*). A tomb supposedly closed over genius; that is, over the life of the secrets it keeps; for this allusion to the library of Yale University, as setting of events that *really* happened, already opened, like the abyss at the bottom of a tomb, all the problems of this library we are in, as if the word 'library', as it stands in the sentence quoted, already contained the space and the future of this library; as if the word were already infinitely greater, more abyssal, than the conservatory to which one imagines one confides it as a particle of the body of one's body of work. Everything that is happening here today was already foreseen, glimpsed, told, predicted, even pre-written or prescribed in the Yale Library in 1964. Date, coincidently, if I may confide in you, when I had the astonishing luck to meet Hélène Cixous, who had not yet published a word. The nearness of this meeting at the Balzar is archived, moreover, on page 55 of *Manhattan*, in the 'list of incipits'. I can therefore, swear, attest, *certes*, that the deed really happened 'in reality', in a reality stranger than fiction, although Hélène Cixous remains responsible for her apocalyptic evaluation of the thing. She indeed writes: '*Like the first time that she had "seen"* [quotation marks at "seen"] *J. Derrida at the Café Balzar. And similarly when she meets Gregor in the Library. Apocalypses that know not what they are.*'

This apocalyptic event in the Yale Library deserves to have been so aptly called, famed, named 'primal scene' by Hélène Cixous: 'The fateful primal scene [. . .] takes place *in reality* [. . .] in the tombstone of a library at Yale.'

The atopic, crazy (in Greek *atopos* also means 'mad', extravagant') topo-logic, the unthinkable geometry of a part bigger than that of which it part, of a part more powerful than the whole, of a sentence out of proportion with the *what* and the *who* of that which contains it and whoever comprehends it, the atopia and the aporia of an apparently atomic element which includes in its turn, within itself, the element that overflows it and with which it sparks a sort of chain reaction, a veritable atomic explosion, I shan't only insist on this when I return to the interrupted quotation. If something is already not obvious, it is perhaps the belonging to literature of the quoted and interrupted sentence, the reference to the library at Yale and to the primal scene called *real* in the very place in which it might have been fantasised. For I have excerpted this sentence from that which one calls in French, again in the strange grammar of a masculine genre, the *'prière d'insérer'* of *Manhattan*. The publishing house, Éditions Galilée, is all but alone today in not making do with *'un quatrième de couverture'* {back-of-the-book copy}, yet another problematic masculine, and in keeping the exquisite tradition of the *'prière d'insérer'* alive. Let us pay homage to one of the privileges and honours of this extraordinary editorial institution, yet another reason for Michel Delorme to be with us today. The *prière d'insérer* is one of Michel Delorme's precious gifts to the BNF. Éditions Galilée publishes *prières d'insérer* of a type never seen any more, *prières d'insérer* signed by the authors, *prières d'insérer* that are not an intrinsic part of the work they introduce but occasionally have great literary value and constitute a genre of their own, works or opuscules in their own right. The *prière d'in-*

sérer I have just quoted is manifestly and legibly signed Hélène Cixous. But it is not rightfully part of *Manhattan*, the work of fiction said to be autobiographical and entitled *Manhattan* that it purports to present or to metonymise. All by itself therefore it raises, reiterates and symbolises the legal problem of limits that we have just evoked. What is outside and what, from the outside, perchance *finds itself* part of the inside as well? I remind you that *Dedans* {*Inside*} was the title of one of Hélène Cixous's first books: published in 1969, awarded the Medicis Prize, published by two other houses, including Les Éditions des Femmes; if I insist upon these editorial data, it is because the coming study of the life and work, as of the whole Hélène Cixous archive (oeuvre and *hors l'oeuvre* or extraneous material) will have to make considerable room for what is not mere editorial circumstance surrounding the work, but a history of this country's editorial politics, hence in truth of its whole culture, its political culture notably, during the past half-century.

(Parenthesis. In the great and incredible atopologic of the *set theory* that I am so doggedly analysing here, I have once again used the expression 'se trouver' {to find oneself, to happen, to happen upon}. To point out that something from the outside, as outside,

61

exterior to a given set, also *finds itself* inscribed in the inside, the bigger thus *finding itself* pre-included in a smaller forever bigger than the biggest, etc. Earlier on, I resorted a hundred or so times to the expression *se trouver*. This syntagm, *se trouver*, interests me for two reasons. First of all, because of a highly idiomatic French usage, untranslatable even, the way an idiom *happens* to be {*se trouve être*} this and not that, in an apparently contingent manner. Secondly, because of the link between the quality of being a genius and the unpredictability of the event, the 'it just so happens' aspect of it, the geniusness consisting in the *happening upon* {*se trouver trouver*} (inventing, creating, inaugurating, revealing, discovering) what happens to turn up where no one had previously happened upon it. I had thought to make an *almost* original remark on this point and to give myself an *almost* unprecedented manner of saying something *almost* new about Cixous's text. Naively I fancied I'd surprise her, so to speak, even if, in passing, I had already noticed, as you may remember, that, as it happens, she herself, in passing, here or there, may have used this odd French locution, 'se trouver'. I even recall giving an example that might seem banal, and, on her part, unthematicised, uncalculated, gracious, practically spontaneous. In her, however, what is most calculated always seems spontaneous and graciously accorded, as if it had just happened to turn up, there on the path, by some stroke of luck. But, once again (once again because I have so often found in her, already seen, heard, read and written down, so many things I innocently felt I had come up with for the first time, all by myself, like a grown-up, and that I had indeed found, all by myself, for the first time, but, without my being aware of it, as so often happens, long after her); so towards the end of my preparation of this talk, when it was pretty much complete and in its final form, it so happens that, re-reading *Or*, on the next-to-last page, I happen upon an occurrence of 'I find myself' that is not only repeated but italicised. As if the narrator, coming to a halt in front of this idiom, invited us to pause and consider it and to take the measure of its genius, of all its lexical, semantic and grammatical resources, this 'se trouver' being able to consist in *se* trouver {find *oneself*}, *se* découvrir {get to know oneself, reveal oneself}, *se* rencontrer {meet} reflexively, specularly, and transitively *oneself* (*se* trouver *soi-même*), but equally well in being passively and unconsciously localised, situated, located, set down, thrown, placed here or there rather than elsewhere, in a contingent, you might even say miraculous manner, a matter of destiny in any case. Without venturing here, as trouvère or troubadour of the language, into the vertiginous semantic history of the word *trouver*, of the syntagm *se*

trouver, of its tropes, of its supposed or haphazard ety-
mologies, without venturing into the Greek or Latin
and German tropes of encounter (*treffen*), I shall limit
myself to reading a few sentences, from the very end
of *Or*. The narrator is ecstatic at the father's letters,
everything must be read between the lines I have sec-
tioned off: 'I never expected such grace [. . .] it is
beautiful. This proud syntax, the uprightness of its
bearing. I recognise the rhythm, it belongs to the
antique affirmation of being [. . .] vital assent [. . .]. I
am utterly delighted: it is a high calm vast impersonal
space *in which I find myself* [this time *in which I find
myself* finds itself written, to draw attention to itself, in
italics]. Without pain, without memory without forgetting without weight without me. But as sublime
joy. I find myself [the second time without italics and
without indicating the place: it is not there that she
finds herself, but simply that she finds herself, she finds
herself for the first time or finds herself again at last:
she finds herself, that's all, absolutely, utterly herself]:
I am adrift on the lips of the letters like a smile [hence,
if, in the end, she finds herself somewhere, she finds
herself absolutely, reflexively, to be sure, but mean-
while she finds herself in a place, namely, as the following sentence informs us, adrift "on the lips of the
letters like a smile"]. Here is the promise of a text
without reproach.'

The *finds itself* is thus both site and event, the taking-place of an absolute innocence, of an antique affirmation of being like a 'vital assent' without fault, before any fault, any guilt, any resentment and any reactivity. Yes, I find myself, yes, here is where and how I find myself. This is also, let me say, my own feeling: that it is unique and I take it as an affirming act of grace, an act of confirmation and of consent, of assent, each time I discover that she has found before me, that which I believe myself to be the first to have found, this or that, all by myself, there where I find myself, and this is, as is well known, in a place and in the middle of a history utterly different from hers, where I find myself finding what she, herself, has *already* found, there where she finds herself. And I don't then feel any debt, any guilt, any resentment. Whatever she gives me, whatever she finds herself finding before I find myself finding it in turn, I owe her nothing. I believe this to be exceptional. And not just in my own life where I didn't expect any such act of grace. In this same parenthesis, I shall confide another similar experience that remains for me hence-forth inseparable from the preparation of this lecture. I had already written, I shall even dare to say elaborated, formalised to the best of my abilities, and even printed out everything you heard earlier concerning the turbu-lence of the jet, of the gé-, of the jet', of the letter *g*, etc., of the *Geworfenheit* and of the *jetée* when, in the course of re-reading *Manhattan*, I come across a passage which, analysing the 'aleatory combination of omnipotence-others', notes the 'secret', again this is her word, of the 'psychical conductors and navigations along nucleotidic vessels unsuspected by me towards the aleatory meeting point where the accident takes place in my sensibility' (p. 121). She makes note of two such accidents, and before the one that leads back to illness at an early age and death from lung disease, here is what she writes: '1. The letter G; the association between the names – the tenderly loved elements of the Georges and the unrecognised name of Gregor; the impossibility in 1964 still for me to pronounce the words *j'ai* and all the other angel-words in *j'ai, gé, jet, gel*, etc., instinctively I always tried to avoid any disturbing contact with G but it is everywhere in disguise in the French language'.

Another example of a debt for which I feel not the slightest indebted: after having, all by myself, associated, justifiably I believed, initially, that which in her surpasses both sexual and literary genre, I came across, as if for the first time, I swear, a certain italicised passage, in *Manhattan* again, which says the following (but any reading worth its salt would regenerate the entire context – a truly endless task):

Everything is perhaps already (played) there in the undecidable definition of the deck chair {la chaise longue}*, a discrete and*

all the more insidious figure for the hermaphrodite: in the trans-
gression of the literary genre; in the transgression of sexual genre.
I should have recognised the demon of the deck chair. (p. 127)

Whereupon, this also needs to be pointed out, switching to roman type, the story slips the word 'genius', with more lightness and irony, into the mouth of Eve, the mother:

– Letters always were your weak point says my mother, whereas I the genius who sent me special letters in which he was talking from London, [. . .] in 1933 while I was in Berlin in a trice I sent him packing. (Loc. cit.)

Elsewhere, Eve again issues a clear-sighted warning against genius:

You aren't capable of distinguishing between a genius and a liar.
    As for me I don't even read the letters of some dubious genius. (p. 196)

There you have Eve, the mother, on the word *genius*. She keeps it at arm's length. Eve is wary of geniuses, she has learned to be suspicious of men of genius. The truth is, these so-called men of genius are nothing but self-styled geniuses, they take themselves for, want to pass for geniuses. Their genius consists in having a stroke of genius at your expense. Not a stroke of true genius, but a trumped-up one.[26] Thus Gregor. Whom the narrator, moreover, accuses of having been devilishly crafty, precisely, in his choice of hotel: 'The choice of Hotel (from the sign right down to the fake [crocodile] suitcase) as decor is a stroke of genius. The little crocodile case is unforgettable' (p. 163).

As for me, concerned to keep the improbable hope of some sort of genius worth the name alive, what would I have to come up with, in the way of catharsis, so as to purify the kind of genius that matters to me, cast out all the wicked and evil geniuses, all the inauthentic ones, if you will? First of all, I'd have to count up all the times this word occurs, in *Manhattan*, at least. They are remarkably numerous and diverse. Without being able to carry out this enquiry exhaustively, I shall be content to signal, for example, the denunciation of a Gregor who, coughing and sputtering in imitation of the great tubercular writers, prompts the narrator to say: '. . . lungs do not a genius make, I thought . . .' (p. 93). On the next page, the same sequence devoted, shall we say, to literary tuberculosis, alludes to the reader who 'loves only tuberculosis' (cause of the death of Georges, the father, I remind you), 'reads Keats for Koch' and cannot hope for 'the author's cure, for this would mean choking off his genius'. Earlier on, we were treated to an evocation of a simulacrum during which the young man went so far as to 'act' a Mandelstam poem unknown to the narrator, with, she says, 'such genius that I would have been hard put to tell the difference between creation and interpretation' (p. 88).

Everywhere, therefore, the idea of counterfeit genius steals in. Genius can be faked, but there is also a genius for fakery. There is of course a 'youthful genius' (p. 135) and the word 'genius' always connotes the origins, the birth, the nature, the nativity, the nation, the upwelling of the beginning. Genius is forever young, in essence. It does not age. But Gregor is a sort of fake young man, the perfect sort of fake and faking genius. There too we find a vertiginous kind of truth, an essence of the truest kind of genius: namely the risk, never ruled out, of an undecidable fakery. Gregor is loved for his genius, but for a genius that, on experience (and what an experience!) reveals itself to be counterfeit, whereas Gregor himself would have loved to be loved for himself, viz. not as a *fake* genius but as a genius of *fakery*. Not a genius of false currency, but a genius counterfeiter. The narrator says it better than anyone: 'I loved him for his counterfeit genius he would have liked to have been loved for his other genius his counterfeiting genius' (p. 231).

Terrifying sentence. Written in the last chapter, entitled *After The End*, and after a final declaration of

love for Literature ('I had such love for Literature . . .')
it seems to put an end, on account of literature, to all
hypotheses of genius. She has loved him for his
counterfeit genius, hence believing blindly in a quality
of genius that Gregor has successfully faked (devilish as
he is) but he himself would have liked to be loved as a
genius of a counterfeiter, thus as a veritable evil genius,
succeeding by means of slyness and an admirable as
well as amiable devilishness, in passing for a genius and
in making himself loved like an authentic genius, the
real McCoy. The evil genius may be he who under-
stands better than others, how to pass for and make
himself loved well and truly like a genius.)

End of this parenthesis that will nonetheless serve as
introduction to what I wish to say about 'genius',
wherever we meet up with it, wherever it occurs, if it
does, and wherever it sets the scene for an event that,
far from fitting into the series, into the *homogeneous*
(the word is apt) sequence or ongoing filiation of a
genesis, a genealogy or a genre, brings about the absolute mutation and discontinuity of all others. How can
this be? I shall attempt to be more precise about this in
my conclusion, from the point of view as always of the
library archive but relating it now not only to the inci-
sive occurrence of a rupture but also to the aporia of a
gift that gives more than it gives and than it is given to

know, both on the part of the gift-giver or gift-givers and on the part of the receivers: the gift given without knowing it, unawares, and thus without acknowledgement, a gift that never seems to be one, to have the quality of genius, and which therefore calls for no gratitude nor any consciousness of giving. Genius is a gift that never appears such, like what it gives. This might be its other secret dimension. Hence the irony that allows a counterfeit *and* counterfeiting genius to give us food for thought on the subject of genius.

One last return to my quote from the *prière d'insérer* of *Manhattan*, at the point where I left off. In it, we already saw the multiplication of the toponymical and topological paradoxes that come along to complicate this sort of set theory that Hélène Cixous's archivable corpus brings to mind. That which I henceforth name corpus includes works published under the heading of literature and texts of all kinds that are neither dependent on nor independent of the literary oeuvre *stricto sensu* and as such. A set theory of this corpus ought to call upon what one might consider axioms of incompletion, a system whose closure remains non-saturable insofar as the belonging of an element to a set never excludes the inclusion of the set itself (the biggest) in the element that it is supposed to contain (the smallest). The smallest is big with the biggest, the small is bigger than the biggest, the litiger contains the tiger, it can be the tiger. Jonas is bigger than the Whale, and the corpus remains immeasurably vaster than the library supposed to hold it. The archive malady is this as well. As with the law of genre which, some twenty-five years ago, in the course of a reading of Blanchot's *La folie du jour*, I attempted to demonstrate, in a text entitled 'La loi du genre {The law of genre}' that what I was then calling 'the genre clause' 'tolls the knell of genealogy or genericity' insofar as the 'mention of genre cannot simply be part of the corpus', and that an 'axiom of non-closure or of non-completion makes the condition of possibility and the condition of impossibility of a taxonomy overlap'.[*]

We have an outstanding example of this in the remainder of the interrupted quotation. We are going to note particularly, and emphasise, the plays on letters and syllables in the engendering of proper and common nouns. The letters of the syllable are *or*, the common noun is *gorge*, the proper nouns are *Gregor* and *Georges*.

---

[*] In *Parages* (Paris: Galilée, 1986), pp. 264–5 (2003, new enlarged edition): 'La clause ou l'écluse du genre déclassé ce qu'elle permet de classer. Elle sonne le glas de la généalogie ou de la généricité auquelles elle donne pourtant le jour {The clause or lock gate of genre declassifies what it allows the classification of. It tolls the knell of the genealogy or genericity that it nonetheless brings to light}.'

Among all the Jonases in search of the Whale in whose belly to perform the rites of banishment in those days was a Gregor, the truly fabulous and uninterpretable character of this attempt at a tale.

One day in 1964 in Manhattan, at the turn of a destiny young but already marked by the repeated deaths of loved ones for once and for all called Georges, between the young woman who loved literature more than anything in the world and the young man whose mind was a copy of the Library's most spellbinding works, the mortal Accident occurs.

This fateful primal scene, the 'evil eye' scene, takes place *in reality* (just as if it had been written by Edgar Poe) in Yale University's tombstone of a library. Sometimes for a mote in your eye, the world is lost.

Afterwards everything happens at top speed for, like the Lovers, the taxi of the crazed rushes down the slope to Hell faster than water throwing itself into a gorge.

Literature as Omnipotence-other . . . (*Prière d'insérer*, p. 2)

In this passage, the syllable *or* orchestrates and organises, starting from the same ovule of sonorous writing, from the same strand of DNA, the relationship *Georges, Gregor* and *gorge*. First *gorge*: at once oracular origin, orality of the uttered sound and deep orifice into which the abyss {*mise en abîme*} rushes, throws itself, plunges, and loses the world ('the world is lost', and 'the mortal Accident occurs'). Next, *or*, a tiny syllable, condenses, there again {*encore*} (*hanc horam* and Cixous is a great writer-thinker writer about time and the hour), yes, *encore*, a little nugget incommensurably greater than everything, for its added-value reminds us not only of an extraordinary book that bears that title (*Or. Les lettres de mon père*, 1997) and which is already an immense poem of the recently exhumed archive (a complete library) of the letters of the father, Georges, to her mother. *Or* {gold} also names the alchemical force of a substance that, at once, undecidably, certifies the unrepresentable, unsubstitutable value, beyond any kind of fakery of that which I should like to call genius and, simultaneously, in the same alloyage and the same alliance, solders it apparently seamlessly to the homo-genising series of genesis, genealogy and genre. This is what I should like to explain, as schematically as pos-sible, in my concluding words.

Génie qui est tu. Silent genius.[27] I believe one must – *certes* – dissociate silent genius {*le génie qui est tu*} from the homogenising powers, of genesis, genealogy and genre, but also from the generosity of the gift when it appears as such. One often says that genius is a gift and that it gives generously in the act or fiat of a creation. But if this were so, the gift would be promptly cancelled out in economic circularity. It would reappropriate itself – with or without delay. Genius that is a gift of nature is not genius. Genius that gives out of natural generosity gives nothing. A gift that knows what it is giving to someone who knows what it is he is receiving is not a gift. It repossesses itself and cancels itself out in awareness and in gratitude, in the symbol, the contract, economic circulation, in the symbolic. Silent genius {*le génie qui est tu*} surpasses both the symbolic and the imaginary, it grapples with the impossible. Genius gives without knowing it, beyond knowledge, beyond the awareness of what it gives and of the fact, of the performative event that constitutes the gift, if there is one. And those who receive from him/it (individuals or institutions) do not know, must not know what it is they are receiving, and which is always more, always something other, older and more unforeseeably new, more monstrously unheard of and inexhaustible, less appropriable than anything one is capable of representing. What I have so far tried to suggest is also that in the gift to the BNF, which the BNF solicited, received, cultivated, gave in return, the giver is incapable of knowing and of measuring what it is that she is giving, indeed even *that* she gives – or entrusts – and the BNF, for its part, with all its distinguished competences, with the incomparable knowledge of its readership for centuries to come, will forever be essentially incapable of determining, and *a fortiori* taking possession of, that which it welcomes, shelters, safeguards, that which it has the signal virtue of offering hospitality to.

And this is good. Therein may lie some quality of genius, if there is any, a genius given and giving. There, at the heart of this alliance, this alloyage, this semblance and resemblance of homogeneity, the thread is cut,[28] and it is the cut of a genius, among all the Gs. Instead of proposing a long theoretical demonstration, I prefer once again to quote a few lines from *Manhattan*:

I didn't look at him.

I was struck by the onomastic resemblance between his name and that of my son the dead but I immediately pushed away this semblance of resemblance, what could be phonetically more removed from Georges than Gregor, that's when he drew my attention to the anagram saying that up until now they'd been called Georges from father to son in the family, meaning his, and that he had been born to cut the cord. I am *the one who sees to* the cutting of the cord says he. He was missing a tooth on the side on top, you hardly noticed it. *Gregor?*

I must have looked at him. I thought of my son whose name is of the earth [Georges, a georgic or geotropical name: Hélène Cixous's corpus constitutes her fields, and

one finds therein a text entitled 'Views of my lands';* one
might dream of geogenealogy or geotropism, and speak
of a comprehensive geography of her work; her genius
is, because of its many languages rolled into one, and
Algeria into France, in algeriance, geographical] whose
disappearance is still so close and already so distant with
what remains of the trembling assurance proper to
orphaned mothers who make believe they don't fear
being swept off their feet with regret. Then, right away,
I ceased turning back, I got up, I headed for the Library.
(pp. 89–90)

On the subject of these few lines, so as to cut short
in turn, I shall restrict myself to two final reveries – or
two suppositions {*supputations*}.

The first, certainly – *certes* – the most risky, goes off in
two directions at once: both towards a situating of
genius *and* towards the ever-paradoxical site of its
expression. In other words towards its address, towards
the 'thou' {*tu*} of its address. By a secret raising of the
stakes, by a hyperbole of irony that makes matters
even less decidable, that which surely points, to my
way of thinking, towards a sharply non-genetic, non-
genealogical, non-homogeneous understanding of

* In *Hélène Cixous. Croisées d'une oeuvre* (Paris: Galilée, 2000).

genius, isn't this described, probably without his being aware of it, by the most counterfeit and counterfeiting genius of them all; that is, Gregor? There's my reverie. My supposition. Gregor, the so-called genius, all unawares, tells of genius. As if it fell to the counterfeit coin to show us, heads or tails, the authentic, the pure gold of genius, in a homage of vice to virtue that leaves us forever in the dark, so far as knowledge and theoretical statement are concerned, about the true essence of genius. As Eve said, 'you can't tell the difference between a genius and a liar'. When Gregor states, in a remark reported, formulated, interpreted by the narrator, that he is the one who *sees to the cutting of the cord* (in italics), is he not thinking, in his dreams at least, of the irreducibility of genius to nature, to *physis*, to life, to genetics, to genealogy, to the homogeneous, to anagenealogy, to filiation even, and this during events of absolutely singular, inaugural cutting, without past and without any possible imitation? With neither father nor mother? Without child, without name and without inheritance, without school, even if everything from which he cuts himself or whose thread he thus cuts gets stitched back up again in the never-before-seen and undecidable event? Genius is not a subject, nor an imaginary subject, nor a subject for laws or for symbolism, a possible subject, genius is what happens. Geniusness is the uniqueness of an impossible arrivingness {*arrivance*} to which one addresses oneself, which is only to the improbable destination of the address – and it is always '*tu*'. A silenced {*tu*} instant, the instant of the eternal return.

Furthermore, the figure of the cut thread or cord or line, whose initiative is here fictively attributed to Gregor by a narrator who knows what she is saying and what she makes others say and what she allows to be said, this cut thread seems, in its very letters {*fil*}, the privileged relationship, the password, pass-key between the narrator-genius and the counterfeit, counterfeiting genius. She herself spoke of this cut thread ages ago, pages ago. Between them, is both the cutting of the thread and a doubling of identity: 'G., she says, I mean he whom I have always called Gregor, I couldn't call him [thus, the one she calls – Gregor – she can't call him, but in fact this refers to a telephone call, a wireless call whose wire can always be cut figuratively, and this telephone, as I have shown elsewhere, is part and parcel of all of the strokes of genius in Hélène Cixous's work as well as in her life], between two Cities, and no phone, the line down on one side or the other, I imagined his state, I thought I was putting myself in his shoes . . .' (p. 41).

My second reverie, my ultimate supposition, so as to conclude finally on the end {*enfin sur la fin*} of the paragraph quoted an instant ago, is that *Manhattan* is a book about the archive and, in advance, deliberately, really and truly, destined for the BNF, for the truth of the BNF; I mean a book made, among other things, in order to speak to the BNF about the BNF, to tell of its achievement and its work, at a time when the author was *already* aware of the alliance ordained, already underway between the BNF and herself. *Manhattan* is a pro- and post-BNF book, and this is one of the reasons, in addition to lack of time and the necessity for sacrifice, for which I have today so clearly favoured this book of a year ago.

The paragraph I have just quoted ends with the return to the Library. She returns without turning back:

> Then right away I ceased turning back, I got up, I headed for the Library.

Not only the whole work, from its prehistory in 1964, engenders itself, enters the world and comes to life in that which over and over again is called the 'necropolitan Library' (p. 43), the 'Library which can be compared to a Necropolis', this 'Beinecke where so many volumes bear witness to illness and agonies' (p. 92), but everything that happens, even the Cause, the *Ursache*, the originary thing, is from that moment on meant for another library yet to come: '*What happens: in the whole expanse of the zone around the point of impact (one does not know exactly where and at what moment God's Devil touched down), hundreds of thousands of traces are deposited as in a sort of library*' (p. 111). The Columbia Library is also evoked (p. 169) and, elsewhere, she describes 'he who first appeared to me on the ramparts of a library' (p. 85). This is not Hamlet holding a book, but Hamlet held on ramparts of books, in the architecture of a library under deconstruction.

Manhattan is beset by the archive, and obsessed above all, granted, by the secret of the archive, that is, yet again, by the experience of being thrown {*jeter*}, of the *jet*, by that which must not be thrown away, even if what one does not throw away, one must hush up: *il ne faut pas le dire*. For instance, this confession or concession of *Manhattan* about the thwarted passion for the archive:

Why have I never tossed out 'the incriminating bits'? I never set foot in either the cellar or the attic, I fear the cardboard boxes, the crates, the envelopes, the compact allegorical beasts big as a good-sized crayfish or an elongated tortoise, belly clad in white skull followed by telephone antennae, old delayed-action suitcases that look for all your life like portable coffins, the miniature,

81

matchbox-sized cake of soap still ivory-white no doubt still packed in its glossy jaundiced paper vest with the logo of the King's Crown Hotel.

Why have I never thrown out the 'incriminating bits', I wonder, I wrote this question as it came, I noted the expression 'incriminating bits' and I didn't touch it. This is a question, this is a fact.

Or perhaps I ought to have asked myself why I had *kept* or have kept the 'evidence'? This would require scrupulous reflection, an analysis to which we should devote ourselves some other time.

To say I have *kept* would be an overstatement, I have not saved, protected, the idea has never crossed my mind.

On the other hand, I've never had the idea of discarding. This is a fact: in the little room in the form of a tunnel that sometimes we call a cellar sometimes a storeroom someimes an archive a few cardboard boxes containing the remains, vestiges, proof pieces of evidence, boxes once filled with wine bottles that end up containing terrible secrets. A matter of many, many letters, drawings, a number of audio tapes, dating from the spring of 1965 as well as a few cassettes.

Might there also be some objects? Dinky little boxes for which I would have given ten years of my life, the last ten?

That the evidence should still be there is in itself noteworthy. (pp. 74–5)

My last supposition revolves around the genesis of *Manhattan*, its time, its length of conception and birth date, its genealogy and genre, if you like. The impatient patience of its writing was, I reckon, haunted by the BNF, it dwelt in truth in the arcane pasts of French literary genius that sleep no more and over which the BNF watches, and over which in particular the BNF's future, beyond its past, keeps watch. The BNF's tasks to come are already turning up to torment the *Manhattan* archive.

On this topic, allow me, in passing, to make a conjecture, another name for speculation or supposition. I shall assume, probably outrageously, its responsibility. This is that first of all, given to or deposited in the BNF, the Cixous corpus, if its depositing or donation is to be meaningful, that is, if it is to have a future, should be at the heart of an active research centre, of a new kind, open to scholars from all parts of the world. As for my aforementioned supposition, namely that the past and future of the BNF is one of the motifs of *Manhattan*, I shall back up this supposition, this *supputation*, what a word, with a single example.

It so happens that a recent, and thorough re-reading of *Remembrance of Things Past* for a recent and unprecedented seminar course led Hélène Cixous to write the following, excerpted from a long reverie on the 'destiny' into which, she claims, Proust 'fell'. Fell {*tombé*} is her word, it is not just any word. Proust is supposed to have 'fallen into' or stumbled onto his 'destiny'. As in all genius stories, it's about the ineluctable chance whereby the dice fall on this side and not that. Between the verb to fall, moreover, to fall here or there, to fall upon, to fall upon this one or that one, to fall upon a destiny, and the verb *se trouver* {happen upon, find oneself}, there is a common mark of contingency which always creates a special case. The *case*, as it happens, is *casus*, that which falls as it falls. It is chance or *écheance* {date on which a payment falls due, term}. Often both at once for better or for worse. One falls, for better or for worse, upon this or that, him or her, as the luck and the crossing of paths would have it. Just as Stendhal, Cixous recalls, owned up to another tumble off his horse, to having fallen off his horse again, tough luck for his horse no doubt, so Proust, according to the expression I made use of to begin with, found himself in place of someone else, and Hélène Cixous says: 'Proust also fell into a destiny, at least, as narrator, in place of someone else. As far as Albertine was concerned he was sure it might have not been her he loved, it could have been {*c'eut pu*} someone else. (*Supu* {*c'eut pu*} he writes in his manuscript in the BNF.) All it took was . . .' (p. 45).

Whether Cixous read this 'Supu' in a manuscript of Proust's at the BNF, as she claims, or whether it's

84

another bright idea of her fiction, I haven't the means to verify and indeed it matters little. This is written in a novel and is first and foremost novelistic. But it is significant that the fiction should have put this 'Supu' in a manuscript supposed to have been happened upon in the BNF archives.

The Supu {might-have-been}, (SUPU) in her shorthand, supposes another possible encounter, another possible love, another possible stroke of destiny. Hélène Cixous has not only evoked, sincerely or not, it matters little, her access to the BNF archives, to Proust's manuscripts, she also points to the fact that 'Proust stumbled onto a destiny' (and all of *Manhattan* and her entire oeuvre consists in showing, in not a few 'primal' scenes, the destiny she herself has stumbled onto, and onto what and onto whom, unending is the list of the singularities that she has either stumbled onto or *come across*, as an English-speaking Proustian would have it). She has especially been struck with admiration, by the abbreviating and playful and learned and precious and *vieille-France* contraction of 'c'eût pu' (SUPU for short) in place of 'cela aurait pu'; and even if she made it up, this comic word that, in four so very overdetermined letters, SUPU, simultaneously bursts out laughing, phoneticises the writing and above all formalises, via this conditional past which thus meets its algebra, everything one might have to say about any contingent event whatsoever. Of whatever happens, of any event, which is in its essence unpredictable and contingent, one says, one must be able to say and indeed one thinks, one really feels: '*it might have been {c'eût pu}* otherwise, it might have been somebody else'. This SUPU is the ABC, if I may say so, of the experience of the eventfulness of the event, even before any alternatives between the performative and the constative. It happens, he or she happens, it might have happened or not happened, it might have been otherwise or somebody else. The one always turns up where it might have been the other, the one that could always have been the other. SUPU is the relationship between the one and the other. In the conditional past, to be sure, which means that the unconditional is truly unconditional, it has happened and the conditioning conditionalities are in the past conditional. They have become unconditional. This is what I call absolute unconditionality, whether it be of a gift, hospitality or love worth the name of love. It is too late to make conditions. One can say 'it could have been another'. But it is too late. The SUPU, this conditional past, is the law of the event, the hindsight of all the 'perhapses'. Even the unconditional could have had other conditions. Once it has happened, it is too late. That's what the unconditional is, beyond all metaphysics of the will. One doesn't decide. This SUPU smacks of genius but it also says something about the quality of genius, the one that we address when we say tu es *tu*. You are *you*. You are silent {*tu est tu*} signifies and magnifies the fact that genius never appears and is never spoken of in the present. No criterion will ever authorise a constative and theoretical definition of genius (as for example, 'genius is this or that, the genius does this or that, creates this or that'); this would be to reduce it to the homogenous, and natural, and ontological series of the genesis, the genealogy and the genre. To say that the genius is in the conditional past, handed over to the 'might have been' of the Omnipotence-other, is to say that it is silent {*il est tu*} but in the time to come, entrusted to others, to all the others of whom the BNF is here the immense allegory, the future itself, genius silenced, you {*génie tu, tu*} will appear for what you have been and who might have been but couldn't be otherwise. Improbable it must remain, I mean forever irreducible to the order of proof. Its truth does without proof,[29] it occurs, it takes place, if it does, if there is one, if need be, without proof, in a place without place for proof.

What I wished to salute, is that which already links the unconditional of a work, which might have been, *certes*, but was not other, and the future, I dare no longer say progeny, who will continue to wonder, as they study the archive, how it might have been otherwise.

Translator's Notes

I am grateful to Hélène Cixous, Laurent Milesi and
Eric Prenowitz for reading the translation-in-progress
and providing corrections, clarifications and inspiration. I am solely responsible for the flaws that remain.
My ambition has been to stay as close as possible to
Derrida's syntax, which, with its use of parataxis, fragments, delay, double negatives, asides and afterthoughts
– in or out of parentheses, grace notes ('*certes* . . .') and
digression (etc.), would in itself be worth close analysis for what it might reveal about the shaping of his
argument.

Jacques Derrida's intertextual comments are in
parentheses ( ) and brackets [ ], as they are in the original text; the translator's comments and alternative
readings are in braces { } where such proximity is useful
and not too distracting; otherwise they are relegated to

endnotes; these are in no way exhaustive; they merely point to some of the more obvious word plays.

Works Cited

Hélène Cixous

Dedans. Paris: Grasset, 1969. Re-edited 1986, Paris: Éditions des Femmes. *Inside.* Trans. Carol Barko, New York: Schocken Books, 1986.

La. Paris: Gallimard, 1976.

L'ange au secret. Paris: Éditions des Femmes, 1991.

Beethoven à jamais. Paris: Éditions des Femmes, 1993.

Messie. Paris: Éditions des Femmes, 1996.

Or. Les letters de mon père. Paris: Éditions des Femmes, 1997.

Osnabrück. Paris: Éditions des Femmes, 1999.

Le jour où je n'étais pas là. Paris: Galilée, 2000. *The Day I Wasn't There.* Trans. Beverley Bie Brahic, Evanston, IL: Northwestern University Press, 2006.

Benjamin à Montaigne. Il ne faut pas le dire. Paris: Galilée, 2001.

Manhattan. Lettres de la préhistoire. Paris: Galilée, 2002. In trans., New York: Manhattan-Fordham University Press, forthcoming.

Rêve je te dis. Paris: Galilée, 2003. *Dream I Tell You.*

Trans. Beverley Bie Brahic, Edinburgh: Edinburgh University Press, 2005.

Jacques Derrida

Parages. Paris: Galilée, 1986; 2003, new enlarged edition.

Hélène Cixous. H. C. pour la vie, c'est à dire (Croisées d'une oeuvre). Paris: Galilée, 2002. *H.C. For Life, That is To Say.* Trans. Stefan Herbrechter and Laurent Milesi, Stanford: Stanford University Press, forthcoming 2006.

Notes

1 **Un génie**: Derrida's question insists upon the fact that the French word *génie* is invariably singular in number and masculine in genre, despite its feminine 'e' ending.

2 *certes*: Derrida scatters this adverb throughout his speech, 'like a trail of white stones', as Cixous said when we were mulling over how best to translate it. *Certes* is an adverb, meaning 'certainly', 'to be sure', 'it is true', and *Certes, un sacrifice,* is the title of the first chapter in Cixous's *Manhattan*; much

later in his talk Derrida will draw his audience's attention to his frequent use of this word and point out that '*certes*' is an anagram for *secret*. We decided to leave '*certes*' in the text, translating it, now and again, as 'certainly'.

3 **tu**: the second person singular/familiar pronoun in French; it is also the past participle of the verb *taire* (to fall silent). Thus '*génie qui est/es tu*' can mean 'genius who is you', 'genius who are you?' and/or 'genius who has fallen silent'. Throughout this lecture Derrida plays on all the meanings of *tu*.

4 **tenir** (to hold): in French one does not make or give a speech, *on tient un discours*. Derrida plays on variations of this expression: *maintenir*, for instance, means maintain or hold by hand (*main+tenir*), and *maintenant* means now, making for a largely untranslatable compression of meanings in this passage.

5 **How rash of me**: in fact what Derrida says, '*Ce qu'il faut d'inconscient*', means, literally, 'how much unconscious' – in the Freudian sense – is needed to presume to hold forth.

6 **multi-directional**: *à plusieurs voies*: in French *voies* (ways, roads, paths) is a homophone of *voix* (voices), hence the shift from roads to chorus.

7 **filiation**: calls to mind *fils* (threads) as well as *fils* (son or sons); hence in this passage and elsewhere

in the book tropes of weaving and tropes of family relationships will overlap.

8 **intriguing plot**: in French *intrigue* means 'plot'; Jacques Derrida writes '*son intrigue la plus intriguante*'.

9 **as it happens**: in French, '*il se trouve*' is literally 'it (he) finds itself' as well as 'it happens'. The many meanings of this French expression are played upon again and again in the text; sometimes in English it will be translated as 'it happens'; at other times by the more literal 'it (or she) finds it/herself'.

10 **nouns . . . names**: *nom* in French means both (or either) 'noun' and 'name'. Thus, further down, when Jacques Derrida writes '*un prénom proper*', one must hear the 'overlapping' of *prénom* (first name) and *nom proper* (proper noun).

11 **the *prière d'insérer***: a (loose) page or two of text inserted in a book and which summarises, in a style between that of an author's foreword and that of a blurb, the book's contents.

12 **Omnipotence–other**: Derrida explains later in the text and in greater detail in his book *H. C. pour la vie, c'est à dire . . .* (Paris: Galilée, 2002), that the word *puissance*, as Cixous uses it, is, perhaps, formed from the subjunctive *puisse* (may, might, let it . . .). Its sense therefore is that of potency. In this translation, *puissance* will be translated as

'omnipotence' and 'might', while *pouvoir* will be translated as 'power'.

13 **given place, led to or provided the occasion**: in French *donner lieu* may mean all these things.

14 **One has no more eyes**: in French '*plus d'yeux du tout*', in which one may also hear *plus dieu* (no more god).

15 **capital-L-Literature**: Derrida plays on the homophony of the letter 'L' and the word *elle* (she).

16 **issue from . . . tissue of Literature**: Derrida writes, '*À moins que Dieu tout-puissant ne soit issue de Littérature, le Tout-Puissant tissue de Littérature*', in which one hears both *ne soit issu* and *ne soi-t-issue*. God comes from, is born of, engendered by literature, but is also the stuff of literature.

17 *L'Ange au secret* . . . **the secret angel**: in French *au secret* is an expression with a multiplicity of meanings, some of which are unfolded in the following lines of the text.

18 **stubbornly hushed up**: in French *têtu, crypté et tu, cryptétu* {stubborn, crypted and hushed up . . .} with plays on all the possible meanings of the various combinations of sounds and syllables.

19 **delirium**: in French *dé-lire,* a combination of the negative prefix *dé* and *lire* (to read). In the next sentence Derrida plays on *oublire,* a combination of *oublier* (to forget) and *lire*.

20 **the crying out of the sacrifice**: in the French of *Manhattan* Cixous writes '*Ça crie: fils*' {it cries: son}, which has the same sound as *sacrifice*.

21 **s'entend à**: an idiom which uses the verb *entendre*, to hear, reflexively (to hear oneself). Thus, literally, someone hears oneself keeping the secret.

22 **with the help of waking**: in French the expression *au réveil* lends itself to the various interpretations Derrida develops in this section of his text.

23 **The dream wakes up**: This passage continues and develops the play on the vocable *rêve*, found in *rêve* (dream), *réveil* (waking), *réveiller* (to wake), *veille* and *veiller* (related to keeping or being vigilant) and *surveiller* (supervise, overlook). Here, '*Le rêve réveille*' may be transitive or intransitive; that is, the dream itself wakes up or the dream wakes (her) up.

24 **seals . . . blocks . . . sentences . . . condemns**: in every case the verb Derrida uses is *condamne*, which can means all these things.

25 **two semantic fields**: Derrida uses the word *portée*, which can mean musical stave and litter or brood, among many other things.

26 **stroke of genius . . . a trumped–up one**: Derrida is playing on the phonic closeness of the French expression '*avoir un coup de génie*' (have a brilliant idea) to '*le coup du génie*' (the stroke/blow of the genius), which is much more ironic.

27 **Silent genius**: Derrida has written '*Le génie qui* est *tu*', which means 'genius which has fallen silent', but the ear may also hear '*le génie qui* es *tu*', 'the genius who is you'. See note 3.

28 **the thread is cut**: in French '*le fil est coupé*', literally 'the thread is cut', but also 'the (telephone) line is cut'. A *coup de fil* is a 'phone call'; phone calls, as Derrida indicates, are a recurring motif in Cixous's texts; a *coupe-file* is a kind of pass that permits one to go to the top of the queue ahead of others. I recall also the connection between *fil(s)* (thread[s]) and *fils* (son/sons), and the cutting of the maternal cord in Cixous's work. All these meanings haunt this passage and the quotation from *Manhattan*.

29 **does without proof, takes place**: Derrida here plays extensively on the different meanings of two French expressions: *se passer* (*de*), to get along/do without; and *avoir lieu* (*à, de*), to take place (of), to be advisable, if need be.